FORGOTTEN TEXAS

Spanish Dagger

FORGOTTEN TEXAS

A wilderness portfolio

Photographs by Reagan Bradshaw

Text by Griffin Smith, jr.

Texas
Monthly
Press

Excerpts from "Ode to the Confederate Dead" from COLLECTED POEMS 1919-1976 by Allen Tate. Copyright 1937 by Charles Scribner's Sons. Copyright 1977 by Allen Tate. Reprinted by permission of Farrar, Straus and Giroux, Inc.

Excerpts from LONE STAR, copyright 1968 by T. R. Fehrenbach. Reprinted by permission from Macmillan Publishing Co., Inc. and T. R. Fehrenbach.

Portions of this book received the Texas Institute of Letters' Stanley Walker Journalism Award in 1975.

Smith, Griffin, 1941–
Forgotten Texas.

1. Natural areas—Texas. I. Bradshaw, Reagan,
1943–   II. Title.
QH76.5.T4S54 1983   508.764   83-9154
ISBN 0-932012-58-2

A B C D E F G H

Texas Monthly Press, Inc.
P. O. Box 1569
Austin, Texas 78767

Design by Larry Smitherman

To Don Kennard

CONTENTS

ACKNOWLEDGEMENTS

The sites in this book were observed and recorded over a ten year period, from June 1973 to January 1983, largely as a consequence of our association with the Natural Areas Survey Project of the University of Texas.

At the instigation of former senator Don Kennard—canoeist, raconteur, and lover of the wilderness—the university's Lyndon B. Johnson School of Public Affairs regularly dispatched teams of botanists, zoologists, geologists, archaeologists, anthropologists, historians, and other students of science and humankind to probe several of the state's most significant natural features and document their findings as a guide for preservation. When Kennard stepped down as the project's director in 1977, the work he began was placed in the care of the Texas Conservation Foundation, a state agency, which has sustained it since.

We are indebted to Kennard for inviting us to participate in that extraordinary venture; to the University of Texas for its sponsorship of the research and its generous permission to republish our personal contributions; to the numerous landowners who so cordially granted us indispensable access to their property; to the executive director of the Texas Conservation Foundation, John Hamilton, and his assistant, Mary Jane Hutchinson, for their patient and unstinting cooperation; to Suzanne Winckler, Paul Burka, Jim Bones, Claude Kennard, and others whose gifted editorial touch improved the manuscript, leaving no infelicities but the author's own; to *Texas Monthly* editors William Broyles, Jr., and Gregory Curtis, who ensured wider public awareness of the project's work by publishing (in somewhat different form) parts of this book in July 1974, August 1975, April 1977, and August 1983; and above all to Dwight Deal, Jim Scudday, and our more than four dozen fellow participants and contributors in the Natural Areas Survey Project: we have seen with their eyes.

R.B.
G.S., jr.

Canadian
Breaks

Harrison Bayou

Salt Flats

Victorio Canyon

Quitman
Mountains

Davis Mountains

Capote Falls

Bofecillos
Mountains

Blue Elbow Swamp

Devil's Sinkhole

Colorado Canyon

Solitario

Devil's River

Fresno Creek

Lower Canyons
of the
Rio Grande

Matagorda
Island

Falcon Thorn
Woodland

FORGOTTEN PLACES

In the beginning, writes Texas historian T. R. Fehrenbach, "In the beginning, before any people, was the land: an immense region 265,000 square miles in area rising out of the warm muck of the Gulf of Mexico, running for countless leagues of rich coastal prairies, forests, and savannahs; reaching out hugely 770 miles from boundary to boundary south to north and east to west, to enclose a series of magnificent, rising limestone plateaus, ending in the thin, hot air of blue-shadowed mountains."

Something of that original Texas still survives in the seventeen sites included here. They are among its finest works of nature, all the more to be valued because they are tucked away in a state dismayingly poor in formal wilderness preserves. They range, quite literally, from the warm muck of the Gulf to several of the highest blue-shadowed mountains, and if they have anything in common it is their seclusion. Though none remains unsullied wilderness in the judgment of those who are doctrinaire about such matters, none has yet been blighted beyond recovery. They are wild places still.

Excepting only the canyons of the Rio Grande and the northern end of Matagorda Island, each is private land. Permission is required to visit, and permission is seldom granted. To a city-dweller the rigors of the trespass statutes mystify, but in rural Texas nothing is quite so real as a property line. Especially west of the Pecos, the Texas landowner and his family live where the landscape is reduced to its essentials, surface and horizon and sky. They live, much of the time, in a cushion of silence, where the crunch of a heel on gravel, a cough, the bark of a dog, the sound of a car two miles away, are audible intrusions. Doors are closed to strangers not because of unfriendliness—a West Texas rancher, once he knows you, is the most hospitable of God's creatures—but because he urgently fears the jumped fence, the knock on the door, the invasion of the silence. These forgotten places are not forgotten to those who own them, and the zone of privacy within which they are sealed can be breached in just two ways: permission or peril.

These natural areas have reached us relatively unscathed because history spurned them, but they are not wholly estranged from currents in the lives of men. One hundred and fifty years ago Alexis de Tocqueville observed the great transatlantic migrations of his time. "This gradual and continuous progress of the European race toward the Rocky Mountains," he said, "has the solemnity of a providential event: it is like a deluge of men rising unabatedly, and daily driven onward by the hand of God." *Before any people was the land,* yes: but before any Texans, numberless others in turn had held it as their own. They rose . . . they flourished . . . they gave way . . . but never did they imagine they would cease to be. Man's migrations are as old as man. To us who lately count the land as ours by providential grant, it is an instructive lesson.

A wilderness portfolio

1

victorio canyon

Victorio Creek

Victorio canyon

One cold dawn in January 1881, Texas Rangers attacked a small Apache camp in the Sierra Diablo twenty miles north-west of Van Horn. The Rangers saw the camp as merely the most recent base for Indian raids by followers of the Mescalero military genius Victorio, whose depredations in the region had reached their greatest intensity in late summer and fall of the previous year. History records it instead as the site of the last Indian battle in Texas—a trivial episode in itself, but marking the fateful moment when the white man took unchallenged dominion over the Lone Star State's contested western lands.

The Indian survivors fled southward with their wounded, pursued by a party of Rangers. Today the quiet arroyo conjures images of Rangers washed and rested, waiting impatiently for their fellow officers to return, wandering away from the corpse-strewn field across the desolate Diablo Plain to a slight rocky rise, there to stand in numbed astonishment at the spectacular scene suddenly spread out below: a canyon two thousand feet deep and five miles long. The majestic power of Victorio Canyon is heightened by the improbability that such a natural drama could be played out silently, without warning, in the midst of featureless desert that gives no hint of what lies beyond. The impact of seeing Victorio for the first time comes from realizing that one has failed to take a true measure of the land. There is an unsettling awareness that eyes can grow lazy with flatlands' predictable dimensions and monotonous probabilities, leaving one unprepared for canyons sliced through multicolored rock and successions of windworked statuary looming on steep walls like faceless apostles around some weathered royal portal. If the Rangers did not see it, it was their loss: the land is worthy of the moment.

Though in area relatively small, Victorio Canyon and Victorio Peak are textbook examples of basin and range physiography. The rugged Sierra Diablo typifies the limestone bank reefs that ring the Delaware Basin. Its prominent kin is the towering El Capitan Reef in the Guadalupe Mountains National Park to the north. The mysterious narrow side canyons resulted from uplift, intense fracturing, and desert erosion. Eastward beyond the canyon mouth a bleached salt basin shimmers through turbulent air. An ever-present wind intensifies the immense solitude and grandeur.

Botanically the area contains climax grama and tobosa grasses with isolated stands of pinyon pine, juniper, and small-leaf oak. Eleven rare and endangered species of plants have been identified in the vicinity, and a shaded fork of Little Victorio Canyon narrows above five thousand feet to a moist, fertile oasis where ferns, oaks, fragrant ash, barberry, and bigtooth maples survive. Found throughout the Sierra Diablo are the native spines of giant yucca, agave, ocotillo, and cactus.

The lower canyon's fauna is typical of the Chihuahuan Desert. Wildlife, after all, is unimpressed by scenery, and neither the vegetation nor the terrain differs sufficiently from surrounding areas for a unique habitat to have developed. Areas above the rim, however, constitute a transitional zone with some of the characteristics of the Guadalupe Mountains. The Sierra Diablo and Victorio Canyon have been inadequately studied by biologists, but apparently the region has been an important route for the exchange of wildlife north and south between the Navahonian Biotic Province and the Chihuahuan Biotic Province.

The most unusual features of the canyon's wildlife are the bighorn sheep, recently restored to a corner of the state that witnessed their "last stand" two decades ago. As late as 1939 zoologists estimated that three hundred bighorns survived in the Sierra Diablo and nearby mountains. By 1956 the estimate had fallen to five. Now the Texas Parks and Wildlife Department has released bighorns into the Sierra Diablo Wildlife Management Area of southern Victorio Canyon and hopes eventually to reestablish them throughout the mountains.

Severe climate and physical inaccessibility have rendered the Sierra Diablo an area of few archaeological sites. Spanish rule left no mark on Victorio. Traces of prehistoric man persist as burned rock middens and lithic debris scattered along small stream terraces above the canyon floor, but the absence of dependable water supplies evidently thwarted human habitation in the area for many centuries. A short distance from the rim, perhaps a half-mile from the precise spot where local legend says the Rangers surprised the last embattled Apaches, the homestead of J. V. McAdoo stands. Built in 1917 by the first white man ever to own the surrounding land, the two-room dwelling served until 1945 as the home for a family of six. Often they cooked and slept outside. The widowed matriarch now lives in a modern ranch house several miles away. Her vivid recollections are a sobering reminder that the white man's presence in the Sierra Diablo has been so brief that its beginnings were witnessed by those still living.

The self-centered arrogance so characteristic of settled, civilized man is impossible at Victorio. He who lives in London or Cairo, Shanghai or Boston—even the man who lives in Houston, Fort Worth, or Alpine—can scarcely imagine the land without himself or his kind upon it, even though he knows intuitively that it once was empty of his people and will surely be empty again. Victorio permits no such illusions. Man's presence—any man's—is revealed for the superficial thing it is. Those who live in the Sierra Diablo reminisce with stories of men who vanished without a trace, sensing uneasily that those stories are symbolic of their own tenuous existence here.

Nothing lasts in this ruthless country. The well-tended McAdoo cemetery stands beside the crumbling homestead, but the hollyhocks are clipped and carried from the ranch house beyond the hills, and the sound of human voices is not heard. Braced against treacherous winds at the lip of the empty canyon, one knows that everything men have fashioned for this land will sooner or later be an archaeological site, a spot marked "ruins" on a map—and probably sooner. Men do not "develop" the Sierra Diablo: they cling to it.

A student of the past has observed that Texas history is a story of racial and cultural conflict. The blood shed at Victorio is a poignant reminder of this insight. But the empty horizon, the weathered homestead, and the dry canyon filled with silences give ironic witness that the land outlasts the men who occupy it.

2

capote falls

The Falls

capote falls

Capote Falls, the highest waterfall in Texas, drops 150 feet from the volcanic rim of the Sierra Vieja seventy miles northwest of Presidio near the Rio Grande. Although its waters disappear into the desert sands before they reach the river, they form a brief dramatic oasis in the barren countryside.

The falls derive their name from a sloping, capelike travertine deposit that backs the lower cascade. For countless years mineral-saturated spring water plunging over the falls has evaporated in the intense summer heat to form this unusual geologic feature.

Sheer box canyon walls rise on three sides, appended with the brown, potbellied nests of hundreds of cliff swallows. Rich banks of maidenhair fern and columbine are moistened by seeping springs and blowing mist. Sunlight rarely penetrates to these sheltered walls where deep shadows and the awesome vertical scale evoke the mystery of cathedrals.

Less than a hundred miles away, the ancient Spanish settlement of La Junta de los Rios (now Presidio-Ojinaga) was a remote way-station for travelers during centuries of colonial rule. Many expeditions passed within a few miles of the falls themselves, yet with the single exception of the wayward explorer Antonio de Espejo, there is not the slightest evidence that European eyes ever observed them. History swirled around Capote and left it untouched, its natural isolation reinforced by the unwitting neglect of men preoccupied with dreams of empire, until 1885 when Luke Brite and his cattle brought a new dispensation to the land.

The stream that convenes the life of this oasis is born and dies in the vast solitudes of the *despoblado*, a stark and angular region that summons to the mind's eye an image of Texas as the world imagines it. Afternoon light cleaves across the broad, mostly dry Rio Grande Valley, drawing the eye beyond narrow stands of willow and salt cedar, shining like some furious beacon with promise of a greener land wet with winter snows where the thirsty river has its source.

Red, weathered Old Mountains of faulted Tertiary stone address the massive Mexican escarpment rising west across the river like the breastworks of two gigantic baronial castles menacing each other across some fancied North American Rhine. In all directions angles lie upon angles, forming a steepness that shuts out civilization and divides mankind into the billions above and the dozens below the savage, sunlit rim.

Through this harsh landscape Capote Creek conveys life-giving water, tempering the desert with foxtails, ferns, and cottonwoods, abrading the rocks to smoothness, comforting the eye wearied by too much masculine country with the gentler ornaments of rills and arabesques. The creek and its feed-springs in the *cienega* above the falls form a unique biological island that fewer than one Texan in a thousand has ever seen. What would otherwise be a desert shrub canyon is instead the home of water-loving ash and hackberry growing over a carpet of green grass and goldenrod. Nine rare, endangered, or endemic species of plants still exist in the vicinity. Below the mouth of the last warm spring, willows and chloris appear; they accompany the gradually diminishing stream through uncompromising country where afternoon summer temperatures average 110 degrees, to the point a short distance from the Rio Grande where it finally sinks below parched stones.

In a region of staggering distances where miles are meaningless, life or death is paradoxically determined by inches. A few steps away from the water's edge, typical dry canyon vegetation appears: prickly pear, lotebush, catclaw, stickyleaf acacia, grama grass, cockroach plant, and paleface rosemallow. Farther back, mesquite and creosote bush visibly confirm the inexorable transition from oasis to Chihuahuan Desert.

The canyon below the falls is a narrow passage through old volcanic tuff. This secluded shelter forms a protective environment for a variety of wildlife like the canyon wren, whose clear descending-stairstep song echoes distinctively within the walls. Seventy-five other bird species have been recorded in the canyon, among them the black vulture, which is rarely seen in other parts of Texas. Twenty-nine species of mammals are known to exist along the creek, of which the colony of rare mastiff bats is perhaps the most remarkable. Mountain lions range the area, and bobcats, mule deer, badgers, and porcupines inhabit the banks of this perennial stream. Unusual reptiles like the all-female whiptail lizards, who reproduce through the immaculate conception of parthenogenesis, and the ornate whipsnake, which may be a distinct subspecies unique to Capote Canyon, help make it a wild preserve of significant value.

Aquatic insects skate across the creek surface, while knotleaf rush and smooth flatsedge thrive in the stream bed. Beneath the shallow, fast-flowing water an occasional brilliant glint betrays a fragment of opalescent moonstone, dislodged from the ignimbrite along the highest reaches of Capote Rim. Washed into the creek, the crystal faces of these gems catch the sun and reflect iridescent blue light to the astonished eye.

Despite the expectation that Capote Canyon must have been an irresistible magnet to Indian tribesmen, European explorers, and nineteenth-century westward travelers, its recent archaeology affords no indication that it was cherished as the oasis we now perceive. Capote Canyon's interest to archaeologists comes from the fact that it lay on a border between desert-adapted Jumano huntsmen ranging beyond the Chisos Mountains and river-adapted Jumano and Patarabueye Pueblo farmers in the Rio Grande and Rio Conchos valleys.

Military rifle shells dated 1915 are silent reminders of Pancho Villa's fellow bandits who raided across the Sierra Vieja rimrock to the Brite Ranch above the *cienega* on Christmas Day, 1917.

Today, the combined impact of man and nature on this fragile oasis is apparent. Accelerated erosion, attributed in part to grazing in the basin above the falls, threatens destruction of the delicate cape. A large section of the capote has broken away since 1964; the plunge pool—fifteen feet deep in 1966—is now no more than a shallow gravel-filled basin. To expect that the falls will remain unchanged in our lifetime is perhaps to make the same mistake made by visitors who admired the plunge pool and the perfect cape two decades ago. Although the past of Capote Falls is measured in centuries, its future may be measured in years.

3

matagorda island

Gulf Cord Grass

matagorda island

Texas is blessed not only with dramatic desert landscapes, prairie vistas, and dense forests but also with the third-longest coastline of any state. Unique in this 624-mile seashore is Matagorda Island — isolated, only brushed by history, curiously detached from the steady throb of mainland activity. With the single exception of adjacent St. Joseph Island, no other part of the coast has remained so nearly undisturbed by man.

Spanish explorers sailed around Matagorda and Spanish cartographers made note of its dimensions. In 1685 the long, grand rivalry of France and Spain first touched Matagorda when La Salle's well-stocked provision ship, the *Aimable,* ran aground on shoals along its northern tip, dooming French colonial hopes west of Louisiana. But not until 1793, seventeen years after American independence, did the Spaniards explore the island itself, and even then persistent mosquitoes and flies forced them into prompt retreat, hurling the epithet "purgatory" at the inhospitable place.

If any figure from the past haunts Matagorda, it is doubtless the swaggering shade of Jean Lafitte. Privateering and smuggling dominated the region in the late eighteenth century. While there is no concrete evidence that Lafitte actually used Matagorda as a base, he regularly plied the nearby waters, and his legends captured the imagination of settlers in the decades that followed. One privateer who did attempt to establish himself at Matagorda, only to meet with mysterious disaster, was Louis-Michel d'Aury. Annihilation of his island forces comprising thirteen ships and over a hundred men occurred in 1817 and has never been explained, although recent historical speculation suggests that Aury's rival, Lafitte, may have cinched his domination of the area in one terrible and destructive blow.

A generation later, the clash of privateers had given way to the purposeful footsteps of European settlers like the Irishmen who arrived with their families aboard the *Albion* in 1829. The first immigrants merely landed at Matagorda on their way to mainland colonies of American impresarios, but by the 1850's settlements had been established on Matagorda and St. Joseph islands. Two-masted schooners provided regular transportation between villages, although the residents (mostly ranchers or shipping entrepreneurs) could, if they wished, travel on a thriving stagecoach line operated by two sea captains.

Few traces remain today of these towns. One of them, Saluria, has fallen victim to a locally eroding coastline where almost nothing man-made has survived a century of hurricanes. Most of the site itself is now under water. The location of another, named Calhoun, can no longer be identified with precision. A Confederate installation called Fort Esperanza has vanished except for a line of zigzag trenches, overgrown with vegetation and detectable only from the air. There is something altogether transitory about the island, symbolized perhaps by the small, now-abandoned United States Air Force base whose personnel (except for a skeleton crew) routinely returned to the mainland at night. Matagorda seems destined to be exploited but not inhabited. It is a passive place, and those who have tried to force it to yield them a home and a living have for the most part left disappointed.

The land they have left is a migrating barrier island, cast up perhaps five thousand years ago and suitable for human habitation no sooner than two thousand years before Christ. In the few seconds of geologic time since it first formed, it has grown seaward nearly a mile, developing sandy beaches of exceptional width—as much as two thousand feet at some points. Thirty-eight miles long and two to four miles wide, Matagorda Island is one of the few areas along the Texas coast possessed of a long beach that is not actively eroding. So few are its visitors that shells and piles of rubbish brought in by the tides lie largely undisturbed along the strand, jumbled relics of human civilization and the life of the sea.

Chains of old primary and younger secondary dunes separate the beach from the storm-built back island, where shell spits, ridges, and flood deltas probe into the shallow bays. The rich broth of marine life could not exist if deprived of these indispensable spawning grounds.

The island's two sides afford a striking contrast of mood. Compared to the rich bayside vegetation around pools teeming with half-seen aquatic creatures, the beach itself seems monotonous and barren. Along the bay the wind is gentle, almost still, and the white birds proclaim their indignation at the visitor's intrusion; there is a human scale to things. On the Gulf the unrelenting sea dwarfs everything, dominating each moment without the possibility of refuge or escape. The beach at Matagorda is for those who are not intimidated by the sea, but the quiet bay is closer to the pulse of life.

The isolation of the island makes it ideal for the study of zoological geography. Restricted travel and the lack of a causeway to the mainland differentiate Matagorda from every other major barrier island on the Texas coast. Since it is not a geological remnant of the continent, it has no stranded faunal forms. It is populated only by animals capable of making passage across the bay. As a result its wildlife is limited but remarkable. Raccoons have adapted to an unaccustomed habitat by living in burrows dug into sand banks and eating a diet of insects and crabs. The rare and endangered red wolf hunts jackrabbits and rodents on grass-covered dunes. Alligators, freshwater pond turtles, terrapins, and diamondback rattlesnakes are established residents, and unique specimens of six-lined race runners inhabit a shell island in Matagorda Bay. Because conditions are ideal for all kinds of aquatic and semi-aquatic waterfowl, most North American species can be found on Matagorda in one season or another. Hawks, turkey vultures, and other nonaquatic birds live on the island year-round. Endangered whooping cranes that winter at the nearby Aransas National Refuge doubtless stray to Matagorda. Bob-white quail, wild turkeys, and a herd of whitetail deer remain from the days when Air Force personnel cultivated them for sport shooting.

Vegetation on Matagorda is typical of the Texas coast. Plants on the low-lying island are greatly influenced by slight differences in elevation and tidal inundation. Sea-beach morning glory, beach primrose, and portulaca temporarily anchor the sand above high tide. Sea oats and long grass ride the shifting dunes, while the back dune region is dominated by dense grasses, sedges, and forbs familiar to coastal prairies. The greatest diversity occurs on the barrier flats stretching across the width of the island between dune ridges and bayside marshes. Needle-sharp leaves of Gulf cordgrass often grow in the company of Indian blankets, pineleaf sundrops, silver leaf sunflowers, panic grass, frogfruit, bluets, daisies, yucca, prickly pear cacti, and Corpus Christi fleabane. Despite the near-absence of trees, there is a wholly unexpected lushness to the island that invites close contemplation.

Owing to the geologically recent formation of the Gulf barrier islands, and to their demanding living conditions, archaeologists have found on them relatively few traces of early man. Matagorda is part of the region historically occupied by hunters and gatherers of the Karankawa Indian tribes. The nomadic Karankawa moved seasonally from the offshore islands to the bays, lagoons, and inland areas, taking advan-

tage of the different resources offered by each.

The ultimate beauty of Matagorda rests not in any biological or historical uniqueness—for it resembles other islands along the Texas coast in many more ways than it differs from them—but in its isolation. The sensation of remoteness, of being set apart from mainland Texas in time as well as distance, penetrates more deeply than other aesthetic pleasures the island has to offer. Should its inaccessibility be lost, Matagorda would be little more than another piece of coastal real estate. Causeways and settlements unmake an island, and it is the knowledge that one is truly upon an island that gives the visitor to Matagorda a special sort of emotional liberation.

It also fires his imagination. That detachment from the everyday world enables him to gaze across the Gulf at night, moonlight layering the breakers, and see the ghostly sails of long-sunk privateers or hear the low voices of Lafitte's lieutenants contriving Aury's doom. Bring the mainland over and the ghosts will leave.

4

davis mountains

Sawtooth Mountain

davis mountains

To the casual traveler the mountains of West Texas are a pleasant scenic interlude in the long monotonous journey across hundreds of miles of arid plains; to the naturalist, however, they are rare remnants of an ancient environment that once sustained vast areas of plants and wildlife similar to those in the Rocky Mountains. Receding under the implacable pressure of a drying climate, that verdant past now survives only on the higher elevations of the Chisos, Guadalupe, and Davis mountains. These true biological islands preserve living fragments of an existence that has otherwise completely disappeared from Texas.

The most significant history of the Davis Mountains, especially the central Sawtooth-Livermore area, is *natural* history. Their importance as a slowly vanishing remnant of Rocky Mountain environment far exceeds their importance as a stage for human endeavor. Their recorded history is so meager as to be disconcerting: despite Spanish title dating from the sixteenth century, they served only as a haven for Comanches and Mescalero Apaches ranging across the plains. The savagery of both tribes made ranching impossible. Not until 1849, when Captain William Whiting opened the first trail through Limpia Canyon and Wild Rose Pass, skirting the mountains and linking San Antonio with El Paso, did the white man begin to make his presence felt. The founding of Fort Davis in 1854 helped secure the area against infuriated Indians, but this outpost was temporarily lost when the fort was abandoned during the Civil War. "Ancient history" in Jeff Davis County carries dates like 1889, when the Bloys' Camp Meeting was founded six miles south of Mount Livermore, and 1903, when the Reynolds ranch began its operations.

The archaeological record appears even less rewarding. Only three sites are recorded within the Davis Mountains, compared with more than eleven hundred in adjacent Brewster County. Apart from a few cliff paintings, pictographs, and scattered projectile points, the only substantial archaeological discovery in the Sawtooth-Livermore area was made in 1895 when the Janes party unearthed a cache of twelve hundred highly distinctive arrowpoints in a pit at the very summit of Mount Livermore. No finds of even remotely similar extent have been made in the intervening years, reinforcing a popular supposition that the site had ceremonial significance to unknown prehistoric peoples.

For the naturalist and the seeker of wild beauty, these mountains hold infinitely greater rewards. Animals living above five thousand feet, isolated from other species on similar mountain ranges by the Plains Life Belt at lower elevations, include some of the most interesting wildlife to be found in Texas. Among the unusual species occurring here are pinyon jays, Steller's jays, Clark's nutcrackers, Cassin's finches, golden eagles, black-headed grosbeaks, Grace's warblers, Trans-Pecos rat snakes, Baird's rat snakes, short-horned lizards, and pocket gophers. The harlequinn, or Mearn's quail, which once was widely distributed in Texas, is now confined to the Davis

Mountains and hovers on the verge of extinction. The only known specimen of a unique species of grizzly bear, *Ursus texensis*, was killed at the head of Limpia Creek in 1890. Black bears are occasionally seen, although the last verified sighting occurred in 1965. Gray wolves once prowled these mountains but are now considered extinct, despite periodic reports of wolflike tracks. Roaming mountain lions have reappeared with increasing frequency in recent years.

The cool, moist northern slopes are covered by montane forests containing plant forms widely distributed in the Rocky Mountains. Madera Canyon shelters a thick stand of quaking aspen. The southern slopes are dominated by pinyon pine, gray oak, alligator juniper, Texas madrone, and mountain mahogany. Cholla, yucca, grass, and dry land herbs dominate the foothills.

Scenically the Davis Mountains have no peer in Texas. Both the Chisos and the Guadalupe have situations of exhilarating splendor, but can either match the sustained beauty of the Davis? The visitor who savors the magnificent panorama from McDonald Observatory on the summit of Mount Locke after a rain may be pardoned for disbelieving that such mellow and seductive country exists in Texas. From a distance the abundant grasses obscure its roughness, leaving only the jagged rim of Sawtooth Mountain and a few eroded volcanic cliffs to interrupt the deceptive velvet surface.

Such vistas make every resident a neighbor. At night lights are visible forty miles away; each new mercury vapor lamp impairs viewing from Mount Locke. Fortunately they still are few, a fact which helps maintain the continued preeminence of astronomical research at McDonald Observatory. But continued subdivision of ranchlands into resort lots will not only mar the perspectives of the mountains; it will eliminate, in a way unlikely ever to be undone, their exceptional advantages as a site for scientific inquiry. If ever a case could be made for preservation of a part of Texas as a wild or primitive area, it is here.

In Madera Canyon, on the mountains' northeastern slopes, that wildness still surges forth to envelop a visitor. The roadless descent, past deep pools of clear green water, has been smoothed into a trail by Mexican immigrants drawn northward by glittering private dreams of El Dorado. But by daylight the aliens are neither seen nor heard. The only sound is the sound of birds. Theirs are conversations punctuated by great pauses, minutes elapsing between responses, inaccessibly strange; it is as if we had stepped for a moment into some intersecting reality where messages are communicated in units of time more spacious and unhurried than our own.

To such solitudes do we come to escape the urgencies of our world; but through them other men descend, soundless and eager, toward the furor we have left behind. We sense this canyon as a conduit to our better selves; they see it as a corridor to riches beyond the dreams of avarice. Each of us wants what he does not have.

5

devil's river

Dolan Falls

devil's river

It is the water that one remembers longest: the river and the sky against the bleached limestone, blue against white, a desert resonance of the Aegean. The springs pour out of the ancient rock, lingering in pools circled by moss, maidenhair, and watercress, emptying into the river. A superabundance of water: dizzying, vivid, pure; ageless water knifing clear deep channels defiant of geometry, crossing and diverging and crossing again; water spun in flumes as exuberant and vital as the festive dances on a Minoan urn; a processional without music.

The spring-fed Devil's River is the last unpolluted major stream in West Texas. Remote and wild, lined in places with steep unbroken cliffs two hundred feet high, it rolls down the southwestern edge of the Edwards Plateau above Del Rio. Twenty miles below Baker's Crossing, a hillside of springs adds

22,000 gallons a minute to its flow; a mile farther on, the waters of Dolan Springs converge, and the transparent river cascades over Dolan Falls toward the immense openness of Lake Amistad.

Only once in recorded history—during the drought of the early fifties—has the river ever gone dry above these springs. Its crises are of a very different order. The barren countryside invites flash flooding, often so abrupt that sudden rises of ten feet are not uncommon. Rises of thirty and even fifty feet have been recorded—battering the tranquil patches of sycamore and pecan along the riverbank, tumbling huge boulders down the channel. The Devil's is a Hill Country river in a Trans-Pecos setting, serene in its accustomed moods but merciless in flood.

This combination has produced some bizarre effects upon the wildlife of a region that is already unique. Dolan Falls is a transitional area for not two but three biotic provinces— the Balconian, Chihuahuan, and Tamaulipan—and the river itself is a key route for the northward dispersal of Mexican birds and mammals. The recurring floods have periodically removed entire species in a matter of hours: blue catfish and alligator gar were both common above the falls until the great flood of 1932; beaver are regularly washed away, eventually to return from the direction of the lake. But the intervals between floods have an impact too. The very isolation of the many shallow springs has encouraged development of a special spring fauna, protected from predators during the long periods of low water. As a result the Devil's River system possesses one of the most varied and unusual fish populations in North America.

The area is likewise rich in reptiles. Among the rarest is the Devil's River black-headed snake, of which only a dozen specimens are known. Amphibians are few, but the doglike cries of the secretive barking frog are well known to ranchers in the area.

Nearly a century of sheep ranching has eliminated most of the large predators that formerly prowled the Devil's River; coyotes have not been seen since the mid-sixties. Mountain lions wandered up the river canyons from Mexico before Lake

Amistad was filled; they come no more.

The transitional character of Dolan Falls' wildlife is matched by its vegetation; botanists, too, see it as the point where three zones converge. Intermingled with the oaks and cedars of the Edwards Plateau are the distinctive sotol and lechuguilla of the Trans-Pecos, as well as the harshly monotonous mesquite and chaparral of the South Texas Plains. The sharpest differences, however, appear as one moves away from the reed-choked riverbanks and the springs; the immense outpouring of cool water is powerless, tantalizingly powerless, to rescue the ridges, slopes, and flats from semidesert grassland. Hillside cactus and catclaw soak up the sun, and lotebush and spiny hackberry sink their roots into the meager, dry soil. The water goes as gravity directs; there is no charity in the oasis.

Centuries ago the Devil's River canyons were green with pine, and the pollen of semidesert plants like yucca was absent from the fragrant air. The past seven thousand years have seen a steady drying trend, its impact on the region's vegetation accelerated by the arrival of ranchers with their livestock. Less than a hundred years after the first white settlement at Del Rio, Val Verde County had become the leading sheep-raising county in the United States; the effect was beneficial for mesquite and cactus—but not much else. The vegetation of the Devil's River bears little resemblance to that seen by the aboriginal Indians who lived there for 8600 years, hunting the same animals with the same weapons, leading a marginal existence in a progressively more astringent climate, and finally, between A.D. 1600 and A.D. 1800, disappearing altogether.

They left behind a dense concentration of burned rock middens in every canyon near Dolan Springs, mute reminders of the powerful attraction the waters of the river held for primitive man. Nineteen rock-shelters have been identified in the immediate vicinity of the springs. More than a third of these are decorated with multicolored pictographs. Although none attains the aloof, otherworldly perfection of the Fate Bell pictographs at nearby Seminole Canyon State Park, the best exhibit the same recurring anthropomorphic figures characteristic of Pecos River art. Archaeologists think cultural influences from both west (Trans-Pecos) and east (Central Texas) may have met in the vicinity of Devil's River, making the region as much a crossroad of human prehistory as it is of botany and zoology.

Cabeza de Vaca, the first European visitor, forded the river in 1535 on his long, desperate trek from Galveston to the Pacific coast of Mexico, but he was preoccupied with escaping from the aboriginal inhabitants rather than with documenting their customs. Among those who passed northward in the seventeenth century, some, like Fernando del Bosque and Father Larios, sought to evangelize the Indians, while others, like Fernande de Azcue, sought to enslave them. Settlements, however, were not attempted until 1808, when a mission was established unsuccessfully near present-day Del Rio.

Not far from that site, John Charles Beales broke ground for his ill-fated colony in 1834. Crop failures and Indian raids hammered away at Beales' dream; finally, as Santa Anna invaded Texas in the midst of revolution, the colonists fled toward Matamoros seeking refuge or escape. Instead they found Comanches. For all but two women and their small children, the Beales colony ended in violent death; behind them, only a church, a gristmill, and a few simple huts remained.

It is easy today to remember only the successes, and to measure the white man's coming with the dry cartographic precision of a frontier line moving inexorably westward. But those who moved the line themselves well knew the failures, knew the lesson in the rotting mill, knew the cutting edge was not nerveless steel but soft and vulnerable flesh—their flesh.

Indian raids continued to plague the Devil's River area as late as 1855. Not until 1868 was a permanent community established at Del Rio, although federal troops had briefly occupied Camp Hudson on the upper reaches of the river after the Civil War. As the frontier moved beyond the Pecos, it left a turbulent lawlessness that wracked the fragile settlements in its wake; outlaws like King Fisher—a murderer seventeen times over before the age of twenty—ranged unchallenged across the brush country. But with an irresistible persistence, civilization nudged its way into the waiting land: by 1878 irrigation canals greened the valley near Del Rio; by 1883 the Qualia family awaited the first vintage from their newly planted Italian grapevines; and by 1884 King Fisher himself was a deputy sheriff in Uvalde.

The transformation became irrevocable in 1883, when a silver spike completed the transcontinental Southern Pacific Railroad at a point near the Pecos. That same year marked the arrival at Devil's River of the two men whose descendants have been most closely associated with it ever since: David Baker, who built his home where the San Antonio—El Paso road forded the Devil's River, a stone's throw from the ruins of Camp Hudson; and E.K. Fawcett, who painted his name on the wall of the rock-shelter that served as his first home near Dolan Springs.

Fawcett's name is not the only one discernible in that shelter, but it is the only one still remembered. The others, faint of heart, soon grew disillusioned with these uncongenial hills and sold their land to him. By this good fortune he became the chief landowner of the area, a figure of reverence well into the twentieth century; in time his heirs became the first family of the Devil's River, dividing his tens of thousands of acres into half a dozen ranches and winning public office in Val Verde County. Until recently their annual community barbecue—a spirited celebration since E. K. Fawcett's days—echoed along the Devil's River with down-to-earth, expansive sociability.

David Baker's son, Walter, resided until his death in 1979 in the old house at the crossing. The legend of Roy Bean was for him no legend; the white-bearded image out of folklore, clasping a tattered Texas Statutes in one hand and a Jersey Lilly beer in the other, was a man he knew in adolescence. Was the old judge honest? "Not too honest." Did he bring a rough but even-handed justice to the dozens of aspiring young King Fishers who booted around Langtry in those raw days? "The outlaws came to him for many things." Our folklore yearns for a white hat to accompany Roy's white whiskers; Walter Baker was among the last to know our folklore expects too much.

In the end, it seems, the character of the Devil's River country owes less to the beneficent water than to the deprivations enforced by climate and terrain. Briefly in the nineteenth century the river indeed bore the name San Pedro—an incongruous choice corrected one blistering day when Captain Jack Hays of the Rangers paused at its forbidding gorge and muttered, "Saint Peter's, hell! It looks like the devil's river to me."[1] The name found favor, perhaps because it connoted the risks implicit where both the land and other men could not be trusted. For most of its history, the Devil's River has been that sort of place.

---

[1] In its wisdom the federal Board of Geographic Names has banished apostrophes from most place-names on the theory that they imply "possession" by the persons whose names are used. The Devil's River having been named for just one devil (the original), we have kept that spelling here. Readers who think this means he is the river's landlord may, with the bureaucracy, delete the apostrophe.

6

blue elbow swamp

Sabine River

II blue elbow swamp

Seven hundred miles from the angular desert fastnesses of Trans-Pecos Texas, surrounded by gnarled woodlands as green as the Amazon, the Sabine River winds to the Gulf in weary oxbows. At its sharpest bend it virtually encircles a narrow, two-thousand-foot spit of Louisiana land, forming an obstacle that local fishermen call Blue Elbow.

The Blue Elbow Swamp, a scant two miles square, extends south and east from this peculiar bend. A short distance downstream its woodlands give way to natural open marsh; and, unlikely as such a thing may seem to the casual visitor who hears the cry of barred owls or watches kingfishers dive into the Elbow's murky depths, the municipal boundaries of the city of Orange are never more than four thousand yards away. Seldom in Texas do the primeval and the modern exist so close together.

Like so many of the state's most picturesque natural areas, the Blue Elbow Swamp has affected history chiefly by forcing history to go elsewhere: unfit for habitation and penetrable even today only by airboats, it is less a theater of human activity than an obstacle to it.

To the south, toward Sabine Lake, the aboriginal Atakapan Indians eked out their subsistence with a diet of fish and brackish water clams enriched, when opportunities arose, by human flesh. Regarded by early European explorers as even more foul and obnoxious than their cultural kin, the detested Karankawa, the Atakapans eventually fell victim to disease and to eighteenth-century Franco-Spanish intrigues. They are known today largely through shell middens left behind from encampments on high ground along the Sabine.

To the north of Blue Elbow, at a more comfortable remove from the mosquito- and fly-infested coast, the civilization of the Caddo once stretched as far as Oklahoma. Archaeologists consider them the heirs of that mysterious mound-building Mississippian culture characterized by precise social orders, complex ceremonial rituals, and advanced agriculture which flourished from A.D. 500 almost to historical times, a strange and as-yet-unexplained echo of the great Meso-American civilizations. But the Mississippian heritage of those who lived nearest Blue Elbow may have been more social than material; the surviving pottery sherds exhibit a design and decoration more like those of tribes known to have inhabited the area of present-day Galveston Bay.

White settlers found the region no more attractive than the Indians had. Orange (originally called Green's Bluff) was established in 1830 as a Sabine River port, its back turned resolutely against the nearby swamp. The Civil War, which might have blazed momentarily up the Sabine if President Lincoln had had his way, was kept away by Dick Dowling's recklessly heroic defense of Sabine Pass, and Blue Elbow was left with no glamorous historical moment to call its own.

Similar cypress-tupelo swamps exist in much of East Texas—or did until recently, when reservoirs inundated most of them—but few ever contained as great a diversity of marine life as Blue Elbow, with its strategic transition from fresh to salt water. Upon an ecological base of shad, herring, and anchovies, the river's predatory fish flourish to the satisfaction of both commercial fishermen and sportsmen. Side by side with familiar catfish, bass, sunfish, and buffalo, others of a more elusive nature teem: the silt-loving, virtually transparent scaly sand darter; two tiny catfish called the tadpole madtom and the freckled madtom, neither larger than a minnow; the cypress darter, which haunts submerged root complexes. The variety of amphibians found in this corner of Texas is greater than in any other region of the state, a statistic that is unlikely to be doubted by the visitor who listens on a summer night to the ragged orchestrations of green tree frogs, pig frogs, bronze frogs, and bullfrogs.

The brackish water supports sea turtles as well as several formidable freshwater species—the alligator snapping turtle (which uses its tongue as a lure for small fish and is itself locally admired as food), the razorback musk turtle, and stinkpot turtles. Every North American species of poisonous snake can also be found, as well as such obscure nonpoisonous species as the burrowing Western mud snake and the snakelike reptile known as a glass lizard.

The bird population is likewise abundant, especially in the winter months when migratory waterfowl arrive; although geese and ducks are the most common visitors, whistling swans have occasionally been seen. Four types of herons are among the most conspicuous resident birds in Blue Elbow Swamp, but the pied-billed grebe (with its ability to change its specific gravity and sink up to its neck) is surely the most unusual.

Mammals are rarer, of course, but the population of beaver and river otters is once again increasing after their narrow escape from extinction at the hands of fur traders in the nineteenth century. The greater menace today comes less from man than from a much closer mammalian kin: the exotic nutria, which appears to be driving out the native muskrat and may eventually affect the entire ecology of the region.

The nutria's counterpart in the plant kingdom is the

Chinese tallow, an attractive non-native tree now rapidly proliferating in the drier domes of the swamp. Underneath cypress and tupelo hung with Spanish moss, often strung with huge three-dimensional webs of giant spiders, Chinese tallow brightens the forest's understory—but at an uncertain price. Lacking natural enemies and competition, it may well crowd out the native species and disturb the eco-system, as its explosive new growth in small clearings suggests.

Recent clearings are the work of nature, not of man; the absence of active timber cutting in the Blue Elbow Swamp seems destined to continue for the foreseeable future. Such forbearance, however, is dictated more by simple economics —the timber is of poor quality and hard to get—than by any desire for preservation. The timber is poor, and the damage already done, because of the logging that systematically stripped the swamp of its finest trees from almost the first day white men came to Texas. As early as 1836, a power sawmill was under construction along the Sabine six miles from Orange, though its builders left to join Sam Houston's tattered army. The tempo of activity resumed and quickened in the twentieth century.

Harvesting first the choice pines, then the hardwoods and cypress, loggers cleared the riverbanks, natural levees, and low hills, floating the logs downstream to Orange, where a thriving mill center arose. Virgin trees in the interior lasted until the end of World War II, when canals were dredged to carry them out as well. Today no significant virgin forest remains anywhere within the swamp; only the gaunt skeleton of an occasional majestic cypress, girdled by the loggers and then left standing when rot or some other defect was observed at cutting time, stands as a mute reminder of what Blue Elbow used to be.

Today the swamp and the Sabine exist together in uneasy harmony, in many ways as dissimilar to each other as both are dissimilar to the urban Texas they adjoin. On the river the hum of activity is never far from earshot, though fishing boats and Johnson motors long ago replaced the antebellum steamboats that once bustled around the sinuous

bends. The river has been appropriated: people live along it, draw food from it, entertain themselves with it. But tie up to a cypress root and walk a hundred yards inland along a piney ridge, and the human signs are gone. Deeper still, except for an occasional fisherman along the lush canals, the swamp seems as elemental as it must have been when the first logger set his saw against his chosen tree. Patiently, indifferently, with a relentless tangled tropical welling forth of life, it pursues its own regeneration.

In a hundred years, perhaps, Blue Elbow Swamp will once again be climax forest; meanwhile it mends. In the spring, wisteria, honeysuckle, and flowering dogwood bloom; persimmons and muscadines ripen through steamy summer days; the red maples, gums, and sumacs ignite with fiery foliage in the long, late autumns. Among them, unhurried, the giant spiders tirelessly spin their enormous webs.

7

devil's sinkhole

The Sinkhole

devil's sinkhole

Picture yourself suspended from a single thin rope, fifteen feet from the nearest land beside you—which you cannot reach—and 140 feet from the nearest land below you—which you can reach, easily. By falling . . . if the rope breaks . . . which ropes have been known to do.

You are disposed, in that situation, to ponder how you got there. If you visited the Devil's Sinkhole with the Natural Areas Survey Project, you got into that situation by strapping yourself into a mountain climber's harness, donning a motorcycle helmet, clipping your harness to the rope, and stepping as nonchalantly as possible off the edge of the Hole.

One of life's most uncommon experiences is to walk over the edge of a 140-foot cliff without, as they say, *result*. This is the same formidable cliff that you first approached a few moments before on your knees, or perhaps creeping along on your stomach: a large, almost circular pit in the shin oak grasslands of northeastern Edwards County, sunk in a self-effacing patch of countryside that effectively conceals its presence until you wander up to the perimeter and notice that it just . . . drops. Very far. As far as a fourteen-story building. Farther than it seems prudent to pursue.

But eventually your turn comes, and you stride toward the hole until your feet tread air. You do not plummet because the rope passes through a boom welded to the frame of a pickup truck parked at the edge of the hole and thence to the rear of a second pickup truck, where it is, you are told, securely fastened. At the very moment your feet begin to dangle, that second pickup is backing toward the hole from its position a hundred yards away, lowering you effortlessly down.

As you descend below the surface of the earth, your mind recapitulates forgotten images out of literature: Jonathan Edwards' spider suspended over the void, Jonah engorged by a colossal gullet. Leaving behind the outside world's insistent glare, you find yourself spiraling silently down a stone-lined cylinder of cool air, aware of no sound except the pulley's diminishing squeak. With each rotation of the twisting rope an unexpected sight comes into view: the hives of honeybees, the nests of canyon wrens, a pair of great horned owls. A colony of some five hundred cave swallows has built nests with the mud that forms below the fern-lined, seeping walls. Along a narrow ledge, a solitary mountain mulberry struggles toward the light.

Aeons ago, the Devil's Sinkhole was an enclosed, water-filled chamber, roofed by a few feet of resistant limestone. But gradually, as the neighboring streams cut deeper, the falling water table drained the sinkhole. Its unbuoyed ceiling collapsed with a roar, leaving a 170-foot-high conical mountain of rubble covering the floor of the 310-foot-deep cave.

Released from your harness, you can wander down this steep-sided mountain into a twilight region of deepening shadows where resilient life forms have adapted precisely to the changing zones of light. A few minutes of sunshine near the top is enough for meadow spikemoss, but farther down, the dim gloom precludes all vegetation. This is the realm of bats: millions of Mexican freetails doze in the darkest corners, emerging at sunset in an awesome rush that can last forty minutes. Fifty-four kinds of arthropods—mostly spiders—scurry, creep, and chew their way across the guano-covered rocks. Occasionally rattlesnakes, raccoons, and other surface dwellers tumble by accident into the sinkhole; the few that survive the impact soon die, leaving eerie skeletons draped across the rocks.

Halfway down the slope, you receive a spectacular reward for the rigors of the descent. Like an immense inverted funnel, the walls around you slant upward to the sinkhole's mouth. Brown rocks give way to green ferns, riveting your attention on the central dome of brilliant blue sky. This tiny circle, a window opening onto nothing but air and color and a transient cloud, is the only visible reminder of the world above—the world from which, moments ago, you peered disbelieving into this Plutonic pit. Now that world itself seems vaporous, unreal. It is a triumph of perspective.

Continuing your descent along the slippery rocks, you soon enter a region of perpetual darkness where overhanging ledges shut out the sky. At the foot of the rubble, several small pools contain the sinkhole's only true cave-adapted species. One, a tiny blind crustacean called *Stygonectes hadenoecus*, is found nowhere else on—or under—earth.

The sinkhole's pools are actually part of a slow-flowing underground stream that emerges as springs along Hackberry Creek and the Nueces River. The confluence of these two waterways, seven miles to the southeast, occurs in a classic Hill Country setting.

Much of the surrounding area, however, has been subjected to extensive clear-cutting and overgrazing. But in the moist side canyons, undisturbed ferns, cedar sedge, and deciduous oaks can be found; nearby, a few Mexican pinyon fight grimly against their multiple enemies: needleborers, porcupines, and an ever-drier climate. Along the floodplains of the East Prong of the Nueces, pecans and little walnut trees have prospered since the days when Spanish travelers first named this the River of Nuts. In still, muddy pools, a carnivorous plant called the conespur bladderwort feasts on microorganisms. The few juniper thickets along Hackberry Creek provide nesting sites for the finicky golden-cheeked warbler, an endangered bird that nests only in Texas.

Proximity to the Rio Grande opened the Upper Nueces to Spanish influence far more thoroughly than many other parts of Texas. As early as 1590, rumors of silver brought explorers here; they were followed by surveyors and missionaries. In 1762 the mission of San Lorenzo de Santa Cruz was founded thirteen miles south of the confluence of Hackberry Creek and the East Prong of the Nueces. Under attack by the Comanches it was abandoned in 1771, and the site lay fallow until American infantrymen returned in 1857 to reoccupy it under the name of Camp Wood.

Once the Indians were subjugated after the close of the war, bold cattlemen brought the "free grass" ranching era to the open range of South Texas. Soon the hooves of Longhorn cattle bound for market rumbled through the winding, narrow canyons of the Upper Nueces, past the site of the modern-day Eagle Ranch that a new century's entrepreneurs—Ling-Temco-Vought—would build as a retreat for their executives.

These tricky canyons attracted more than their share of desperadoes and cattle thieves: John Wesley Hardin, Ben Thompson, and Bill Longley in the 1870's; the Black Jack Ketchum Gang, the Pegleg Gang, and Butch Cassidy's Hole in the Wall Gang in the 1880's and 1890's. Long past the time when law and order prevailed elsewhere in Texas, the Upper Nueces persisted as an outlaw sanctuary.

There is no record that Butch Cassidy and his partners ever paused to gape at the Devil's Sinkhole; their enthusiasms plainly took a different turn. But the local bandits could not have been entirely absent from the mind of a man named H. S. Barber, who managed to descend the Sinkhole and carve his name at the bottom in 1889, temporarily leaving his rope

ladder—and thus his only means of returning—at the mercy of whoever happened by.

If you follow him today, you share his absolute dependence on the good will of anyone on the rim; there is no way to escape unaided. But paradoxically, as you look up to that tiny window, the ties that join you to your fellow men on the surface seem altogether insubstantial. You are merely a particle in the earth's crust, swallowed. You could be anywhere. Not until you reattach yourself to the harness and spiral upward out of the clammy air into the plateau's scalding light do you restore your conventional perspective.

The disorienting shock soon fades. You walk away, not wishing to look back down. The pickup driver turns; you wave: "Thanks! Great entertainment."

8

canadian breaks

The Breaks

canadian breaks

Only a geologist could love it. An archaeologist, sifting through its stones to find a weapon that might have ricocheted against a mammoth's skull, can feel excitement for the place; but love? A historian can revere the legions of men who brought their folkways to it and then moved on, leaving it for others; but—panoramic, technicolored—it remains a stage and not an object of affection. A zoologist, a botanist, can search in vain for the extraordinary find, the unexpected living thing that brings a quickening of the pulse. But the geologist, standing in windy solitude, sees something different: a contorted badlands of canyons, buttes, and mesas. Perhaps—depending on his mood and the play of light against the cliffs of multicolored shale—he might even say he loves it.

A snicker would be inappropriate: the geologist is accustomed to fixing his ardor on places that other scientists find devoid of interest, sites whose very barrenness best exposes the uplifts and erosion that made them what they are. The Breaks of the Canadian River—a landscape of almost biblical desolation—suit his purpose admirably. From the level plain of the Llano Estacado northwest of Amarillo they appear first as slight canyons, then as whole eroded valleys lined with vivid colored rock, expanding in scale and majesty as they approach the sandy riverbed. Along the dry arroyos one often finds cut banks composed of five hundred or more strata, each perfectly identifiable and distinct even if no more than one-sixteenth of an inch thick, a veritable library of sedimentary history. Higher up, these sandstones give way to several hundred feet of Triassic shales whose wine-hued purples, maroons, and reds are interspersed with white and yellow. Still higher, other sandstones and resistant shales cap the buttes and mesas, leaving grass-topped sentinels to guard the empty valleys.

Few places anywhere belong so completely to the wind. It whines continuously through the canyons at an average velocity of sixteen miles an hour, scattering microscopic red dust over everything and torturing shrubs into parodies of bonsai. The wind is a moody sovereign, intensifying not only the torrid summer temperatures that reach as high as 109 degrees but also the bitter winters as cold as 18 below. It dries the valley floors, leaving salt pans in place of water, and sculpts every ridge and crevice of the rocky walls. There is war here between wind and stone, and the wind is winning.

The sparse vegetation consists primarily of mesquite, bristle grass, skunkbush, grama, and galleta. Near the bone-dry Canadian River, salt cedars cluster in a dense canopy; on the southern Breaks a stand of juniper survives; and along the side canyons, occasional cottonwoods afford protective shade.

It is not an inviting place for man or beast. Reptiles like the collared lizard, the checkered whiptail, and the diamondback rattlesnake nevertheless find it congenial, as do coyotes; and birds like Bullock's oriole regard the cottonwoods as splendid nesting sites. Indeed, the trees may well be the most important zoological aspect of the Breaks, offering valuable shelter that is lacking elsewhere in the Llano Estacado.

The history of the Canadian River country is as layered as the rocks themselves. One human society after another has flowed across the plains, leaving behind rich artifacts and richer legends.

The earliest traces suggest that primitive men armed only with atlatls pursued bison, camels, and mammoths here as long ago as 18,000 B.C. Later, and more ingeniously, they drove their quarry into box canyons for the kill, or stampeded the beasts over some convenient precipice.

The region's most impressive prehistoric remains, however, date from the era of the mesa-dwelling Indian farmers who occupied the Breaks from about A.D. 1100 until their civilization was destroyed by drought about 1500. Their architecture and pottery are among the most impressive to be found in Texas. In the Canadian River valley they cultivated pumpkin, maize, beans, and squash with crude stone hoes and other tools, living in communal apartment buildings atop the nearly inaccessible mesas. The finest surviving example of their culture, Landergin Mesa, stands a few miles south of the river. It is almost entirely covered by the remains of a rectangular stone structure comprising numerous rooms; to one side, manos and grinding slabs can still be found. Situated 180 feet above the valley floor and protected by sheer sandstone walls, it offered proximity to farming land, security from marauding enemies, and unobstructed views of distant hunting grounds.

As the climate of the Canadian Breaks grew drier in the sixteenth century, a new tribe of buffalo hunters—the nomadic Jumanos—infiltrated these abandoned farms. They survived by trading dried meat and hides with their more settled cousins to the west, and it was they whom the Spanish conquistadores first encountered in their futile quest for gold.

Coronado's expedition passed well south of the Breaks, entering Palo Duro Canyon before turning north toward Oklahoma. Not until 1601, when Juan de Oñate followed the north side of the Canadian River searching for the fabled city of Quivira, did European influence arrive. The land was fresher then: "rich in fruits, particularly of infinite varieties of plums, the fruit more numerous than the leaves," Oñate reported to the king of Spain. His men nibbled wild grapes and drank from the many springs that bubbled forth along the Breaks; around them, countless buffalo savored the limitless grass.

To this tranquil country the Apaches soon came, thundering on horseback from the northern plains. By 1650 they had convincingly overthrown the Jumanos and made themselves masters of a territory Spanish in name only. But their domination too was only temporary. From ancestral homes along the Yellowstone River in the northern Rockies, the Comanches poured southward like an equestrian plague, annihilating opposition. By 1725 the land was theirs, though massacres continued as long as straggling Apaches could be found.

A Comanche peace descended upon the Canadian Breaks, not to be broken until 1849 when well-armed convoys of gold-seekers burst through toward California, leaving in their wake disease and slaughtered buffalo. The sullen Indians first traded with, then fought, the interlopers. For a while, amid the distractions of the Civil War, they were successful. It was then, amazingly enough, that Mexican sheep ranchers moved undisturbed into the Breaks, building stone masonry "plazas" and practicing a sly coexistence. The remains of one such plaza can be seen today in a grassy area between Landergin Mesa and the dry riverbed, a weathered heap that once housed an isolated family who found—temporarily—the secret of cooperation with the feared Comanches.

Federal troops finally overcame the Indians, leaving Americans free to descend upon the unspoiled plains where grass, they said, grew tall as wheat. Events moved with kaleidoscopic quickness after Mackenzie destroyed the Comanches' horses at Tule Canyon in 1874. Buffalo hunters like the Mooar brothers came and went, leaving by 1879 an eerie silence and a million shaggy corpses. Cattlemen like Goodnight, Pierce, and Loving followed; Pat Garrett and Billy the Kid walked the streets of Tascosa, the jerry-built supply town that sprouted a few miles east of Landergin Mesa. The land, bruised by too many cattle, began to change; grass gave way to gullies; and mesquite seeds, undigested by the grazing herds, sprouted into thickets of thirsty trees that sapped the topsoil dry. In 1886 and 1887, successive drought and polar winter dealt the cattlemen a deadly blow. The Canadian Breaks would never be the same.

By 1887 barbed wire, windmills, and the railroad's arrival combined to put an end to open range. The great trails, like the Jones and Plummer Trail that crossed the Canadian at Tascosa, were doomed. Even the town itself was passed by, crumbling into ruins while upstart Amarillo prospered.

Later, oilmen came, and ranching accommodated itself to the unromantic reality of feedlots. A hundred years after Mackenzie opened this land to settlement, the raucous pioneer world had been replaced by orderly conservatism. Less than 125 years after white men feared to set foot here, 300,000 Americans occupy the upper Panhandle.

Few, however, venture into the Canadian Breaks, which have distilled into themselves the spacious solitude that once spread hundreds of miles beyond their jagged canyons. The many springs are gone, victims of the distant irrigation that has sucked the groundwater away. The land is strangled with mesquite, a persistent legacy of overgrazing. The last wave of human civilization to cross the Breaks has scraped them clean; now there is nothing left but the wind and the sculptured rocks.

At night, from the air, the High Plains sparkle with lights, but the Canadian Breaks lie apart: lonely, brooding, dark.

On the windswept coast of North Africa, near the shabby Libyan town of Tobruk, a stolid windowless building dominates a barren hill. The wreaths inside its bronze doors are gray and withered; only their ribbons are bright. At the four corners of its inner courtyard, the thick walls of somber brown stone are interrupted by iron grillwork, through which one can see . . . nothing but empty desert.

This building is the mausoleum of six thousand German soldiers who fought with Rommel and never crossed the Mediterranean again; their bodies are piled within the walls that bear their names. Weeks pass without a visitor. One looks at the tomb and wonders that men should have come so far from home to die, and to such desolation.

On the other side of the world, the Canadian Breaks have that same charnel loneliness: the same dry grit in the air, the same incessant wind speaking in the same low moan. One looks across the Breaks from Landergin Mesa and for a moment the whole human pageant is arrested: a paleo-Indian, arm upraised in vain to block the mammoth's tusk; the mesa-dwelling farmer, shaking the last grains from the scorched maize that nourished his ancestors; the aging Comanche, retelling by firelight the legends that were born in Yellowstone; the bearded Kansas émigré, staring at the frozen carcasses of his cattle and knowing that the ice has killed his dreams as well. Like Tobruk, those who came here called better places home, but their monument is as insubstantial as the red dust that drifts without repose. The pageant has passed across and left behind nothing—except the stones.

The geologist smiles. He knows.

9

colorado canyon

Rio Grande

colorado canyon

Colorado Canyon is the first, and shortest, of the Big Bend's monumental canyons. Its entrance 28 miles southeast of Presidio brings to a close the broadly majestic, even extravagant, valley through which the river has passed for most of its length below El Paso. Beginning at Colorado Canyon the Rio Grande struggles to find a path to the sea.

Aeons ago, the volcanic rock at its entrance was a natural dam holding back a vast lake within the Presidio and Redford bolsons. Sediments carried by rainfall runoff in the ancestral Rio Conchos and by snowmelt in the ancestral Rio Grande gradually filled the basin until the dam was breached. With excruciating slowness, the waters began to etch a downstream path, excavating canyons that have steadily deepened over time and surrounded the river with a scenic badlands of eroding tributaries.

The barrier broken by the river proved more difficult for man to overcome. Colorado Canyon, together with a formidable dome of rhyolite porphyry two miles downstream known as Big Hill, impeded human traffic across this region from prehistoric times until a road was blasted through in 1961. Archaeological evidence shows that the settlements of Indians who practiced agriculture and manufactured pottery throughout much of the American Southwest cease abruptly near Redford; not a single ceramic sherd has been discovered around Colorado Canyon or beyond. Similarly, the area's lithic artifacts do not correspond to types associated with the Big Bend, the Davis Mountains, or any downstream culture, prompting archaeologists to speculate that whatever primitive peoples lived here were an isolated society confined to the Colorado Canyon–Fresno Canyon vicinity.

Presidio is, of course, rich in both Spanish and nineteenth-century American history; but its commerce flowed along a north-south line through the interior, avoiding the river and Colorado Canyon. Efforts to find a safe passage from San Antonio through Presidio to El Paso came to grief in the Hays-Highsmith expedition of 1848 and the Whiting expedition of 1849. When the connection was finally made it crossed overland, far from the river.

The spectacular entrance to Colorado Canyon was viewed—on those rare occasions when it was viewed at all—as the gateway to an unknown region until 1852, when William Emory's scientific reconnaissance party passed through. His was the first serious attempt to chart the hidden reaches of the river, if one discounts the ludicrous Love expedition of 1850, which tried to reach El Paso from Rio Grande City in fifty-foot flat-bottomed boats, and the saner Smith expedition, which managed to navigate upstream to a point eighty miles above the confluence of the Pecos. The work begun by Emory was not resumed until 1899, when geologist Robert Hill, with far greater expertise, mapped the entire river system from Presidio to Langtry. In the interim and until quite recent times, man was a stranger to the swirling water and the sunsets refracted beneath the craggy walls; Colorado Canyon slept the deep primeval sleep of wilderness unobserved.

Today it is easily negotiable by canoe or kayak, especially during the spring or fall when water levels are most likely to be favorable. Access is almost effortless; the Camino del Rio, the new river road, links the two points with a ten-minute drive, and the land (still private) slopes gently to the river. Between these points the road veers out of sight behind high hills, granting the lucky canoeist total solitude for the duration of his run. Few wild rivers anywhere are so well adapted to satisfy one's every wish.

At normal water the trip takes half a day. Enough rapids exist to keep the adventure lively, but the canoeist can still find time to admire the geologic drama unfolding around him. Through immense faulted blocks of volcanic lava, tuffs, and ash the Rio Grande cuts, rolling past massive columnar jointed cliffs of weathered orange ignimbrite. In the deepest part of the canyon the walls rise eight hundred feet above the water's edge.

A narrow, steep side canyon enters from the left. This is Closed Canyon, a tributary carrying outwash from the Bofecillos Mountains. The broad-tailed hummingbird has been seen nesting here, as has the prairie falcon; and the rare perennial *Machaeranthera gypsophila* displays its showy white and yellow flowers after a drenching rain.

The slender green band of vegetation along the river is dominated by plants foreign to the botany of the Chihuahuan Desert: Bermuda grass and salt cedar, both native to India; carrizo, an Asian grass; and South American tree tobacco, beloved by the six species of hummingbirds known to visit here. But the sandy banks of Colorado Canyon also play host to such familiar domestic plants as mesquite, seep-willow, canyon grape, sunflower, and poison ivy.

Bats and birds use the river as a corridor through otherwise inhospitable terrain. Multitudes of migratory water-fowl pay annual visits; others arrive and depart with unpredictable irregularity. Birders' records are replete with more than 150 different species, and twice that many are thought to put in an appearance during any given year.

As the river emerges into lowlands between the canyon and Big Hill, startled canoeists have occasionally encountered equally startled bears, who turn tail and head back to the sanctuary of the Mexican mountains. Much more common, however, are the mysterious Mexican beavers, who do not build dams or lodges as proper bourgeois beavers do, but who nevertheless often wreak havoc with their destructive gnawing of valuable shade trees. Muskrats are gradually returning to their former range along this portion of the river; several have been sighted upstream from Lajitas, and they may already have reestablished themselves as far west as Big Hill. Three rare snakes—the Texas lyre snake, the Trans-Pecos rat snake, and the gray-banded king snake—are among the many species known to inhabit Big Hill.

Construction of Camino del Rio set in motion forces that could destroy Colorado Canyon's fragile ecology. Commercial animal dealers from as far away as California now flock to the highway to capture and eventually sell rare specimens of wildlife, particularly the gray-banded king snake, which fetches more than $100 in the pet trade. Fishermen have already introduced one foreign species to the river, the barred tiger salamander; and they have been known to smash the dry mud nests of cliff swallows and use the baby birds as bait.

The greatest threat to Colorado Canyon's survival comes, however, from an altogether different source: the river itself. Even in Spanish days the Rio Grande above La Junta occasionally ran dry; modern dams have simply made an intermittent condition almost permanent. For decades the Rio Conchos has supplied the flow that kept the "Rio Grande" below Presidio alive. The riparian existence of Colorado Canyon and the others in Big Bend—Santa Elena, Mariscal, Boquillas—depends on rains in the Sierra Madre Occidental, transported by the Conchos across the arid reaches of northern Mexico. But dams built for irrigation in the mountains southwest of Chihuahua have increasingly begun to stanch that flow. Although a minimum supply of water is presently guaranteed by international treaty, the desperate agricultural needs of Mexico's burgeoning population may soon require all

the water the Conchos can provide. Treaties have been known
to yield to less. If the alternative is hunger, Colorado Canyon
may be fated to become, before the end of this century, a dry
arroyo evidencing the fitfulness of man's rapport with nature.

10

bofecillos mountains

Upper Wylie Mesa

bofecillos mountains

Between Redford and Lajitas a line of high bluffs guards the Texas side of the Rio Grande. Rising steeply to promontories nearly two thousand feet above the river's edge, then changing to rolling high country speckled by the dark peaks of five-thousand-foot mountains, this is the front line of the Bofecillos Range. Twenty million years ago, when the region we now know as the border was a place of glowing cones and vents and smoke and ash and magma, volcanoes built up the Bofecillos; later, when the Rio Grande broke through the nearby Redford Bolson and began to carve its channel to the Gulf, erosion gnawed away at the adjacent mountains, incising them with tributary canyons.

Today one can drive (albeit with difficulty) to the very lip of one of these high bluffs and look out upon a Texas shaped by earth, wind, and water only; not by man. From the crest of Upper Wylie Mesa one can gaze for fifty miles, past steep striated canyon walls of red and white and brown and yellow, above the talus slopes and trickling water of Tapado Canyon, over the brushy solitude of flat-topped Burro Peak, to the meandering Rio Grande beyond. The only sign of civilization is a speck of irrigated green in the distant Redford valley. From Wylie Mesa it seems less an intrusion than a confirmation of man's insignificance in the scheme of things. One comes to the rim at sunset and finds Texas when it was new.

The Bofecillos remain sufficiently unspoiled that a visitor can still find manos that have lain untouched since they were set aside by Indian hands perhaps four hundred years ago. Seven canyons—Bofecillos, Auras, Las Burras, Tapado, Rancherias, Panther, and Madera—pierce the mountain flanks from west and south; in them, and in the high country above, the dense aggregation of archaeological sites shows what powerful attractions the Bofecillos held for prehistoric man. Water was evidently foremost: seeps and springs are common, especially in the canyon bottoms. Security was doubtless another: rock-shelters were a welcome protection against the elements and possibly against enemies as well. The lithic debris associated with these shelters is often substantial, forming what amounts to cultural talus slopes. Sandals, quids, and animal remains have occasionally been found—a reminder that the clans subsisted by hunting small game and processing tuberous plants. A dense concentration of ovenlike hearths near Rancherias Springs gives a clue to the methods they may have used. Simple patterns of life associated with Archaic times seem to have persisted with little change well into the seventeenth century.

Pictographs are found in Bofecillos, Auras, and Las Burras canyons—but not, so far as is known, in the four canyons farther east. They reappear in Fresno Canyon, which forms the eastern limit of the Bofecillos Range, but are absent again in the adjoining Solitario. Depicting abstract geometric designs as well as lifelike figures in multicolored pigments, they are a puzzle to archaeologists not only for their geographical distribution but also for their distinctive style; they may, in fact, constitute an isolated form unique to the Bofecillos Mountains.

The reliable water supplies that attracted prehistoric man owe their existence to a fortunate geologic accident. Following deposition of Cretaceous sediment and the coarse-grained Jeff Conglomerate, repeated volcanic eruptions left alternating layers of hard and soft strata in the Bofecillos Mountains. These layers—the Chisos Formation, the Mitchell Mesa Tuff, local ash and lava flows from the Bofecillos Vent, and the Santana Tuff—were penetrated by hot magma, leaving dikes and laccoliths; later they were torn by faults. The simple result of this complex activity was the creation of numerous aquifers in porous zones around the resistant lava flows, aquifers generously charged from rainfall on the high summits of the Bofecillos Mountains. From them, water emerged as seeps and springs throughout the region.

This was the Bofecillos that the Indians knew; it is also the Bofecillos we know today. That fact is more remarkable than it sounds. Throughout West Texas, springs that flowed copiously as short a time as fifty years ago are dead, dried up when the water table was lowered by widespread drilling of wells for ranching and agriculture. Those in the Bofecillos have escaped this fate—not because the overlying land has been used differently (heavy grazing has been practiced there for decades) but because the water for livestock has been obtained differently. Instead of drilling wells at remote locations across the immense Big Bend Ranch, its former owners Edwin and Manny Fowlkes erected windmills to pump surface water from the dependable but inaccessible springs to the grasslands on the mesas. After World War II they obtained enormous quantities of surplus pipe and expanded the system across the Bofecillos to Fresno Canyon and the Solitario. At its peak, before they sold the ranch in the 1950's, their implausible, extraordinary pipeline system stretched and twisted for hundreds of miles, using spring water and the yield from one or two good wells instead of depleting the aquifers artificially. A sizable portion of the system remains operational today. Consequently, the Bofecillos watershed still functions as it has for centuries.

The Bofecillos Mountains are more than a geologic laboratory where students can observe in fine detail the internal layering of volcanic action; they are an assemblage of fragile oases. These mountains hold their share of rare and relict plants and animals, but in their entirety they are more: they are, themselves, a relict region.

Like so much of the Big Bend country, theirs is a value beyond measurement. They are the last surviving huge wild part of Texas. In a sense where metaphor comes closer to reality than logic, they are the only "true" Texas that remains. To explore the canyon below Rancherias Springs is to touch for a moment the frontier experience shared, in different landscapes and under different climates, by those who subdued the Piney Woods, the Hill Country, the Staked Plains, and all the other stern resisting wilderness a century and more ago. The utter solitude, broken by birds and insects only, reconstructs the mood of limitless possibility and vague foreboding that faced everyone who pushed the frontier westward. To experience this lonesome, unbeaten land is to bridge the gulf that separates us from those ancestral settlers, letting us learn physically what we can never fully learn from books and legends.

11

fresno creek

Arroyo Segundo

fresno creek

The search for water is the one abiding constant of human life in Trans-Pecos Texas. It has dictated the routes of travelers, the sites of towns, and the likelihood of wresting a living from an obstinate land. Because the oases are so few they have been treasured immemorially. It seems inconceivable that any of them, once discovered, could ever be forgotten.

Yet that has been the fate of the nameless perennial stream that flows through a side canyon known as Chorro in the uplands north of Redford. Fed by springs bubbling out of basalt porphyry in the eastern Bofecillos Mountains, it drops through two cascades one hundred feet and thirty feet in height before coasting lazily through a reed-choked bed toward Fresno Canyon and the Rio Grande. The stream must have been known to prehistoric man, and it was certainly known to early settler C. H. Madrid, who came there in the 1870's and

127

eventually built a ranch house on a fertile terrace near its banks. But in time the Madrids moved to Redford, taking the memory of Chorro Canyon with them. When a topographic survey team "discovered" the stream and waterfalls in 1970, the news came as a surprise to all but the Madrid family and a few hands on the Big Bend Ranch.

The larger waterfall, christened Upper Madrid Falls, offers a miniature forest of lush vegetation that may be the closest thing to Eden that West Texas will ever know. Cottonwood, willow, oak, and ash fill the narrow canyon, cloaking the splash pool in almost constant shadow. The stream itself slides in a diamond-shaped pattern down a rock face nicknamed the pedestal, passing rare columbine, wild rye, and maidenhair along the way. Replenished by underwater springs, it flows through a thicket of crumbling logs and grapevines to the lesser lower falls. Animal life that could not last more than hours in the adjacent desert survives trapped, if that is the word, amid the cool and damp perpetual green. The secretive Madrean cliff frog, whose cry is heard only when the humidity meets its satisfaction, is found here; so, too, are the canyon treefrog and the rare, relictual Trans-Pecos copperhead.

This fragile ecological island continues to exist only because the Chorro watershed above the falls is small enough to escape the tumultuous flash floods that regularly rip the vegetation from other Big Bend canyons, including Fresno Canyon itself, into which Chorro Canyon empties.

Despite the floods, water is Fresno Canyon's special wealth. This mile-wide valley separates the Solitario from the Bofecillos Mountains, carrying runoff from each into the Rio Grande. Fresno Canyon's two sides are dramatically different, not only in their biology but in their geology as well. The eastern, or Solitario, slope consists of steeply dipping, pale Cretaceous limestone. Devoid of natural surface water, it supports an environment indistinguishable from the Chihuahuan Desert norm. The western, or Bofecillos, slope is built of alternating hard and soft volcanic rocks; groundwater trapped between the layers emerges to dissect the dark cliffs with mesic canyons like Chorro. Other springs, always from the west, form tiny ponds within Fresno Canyon proper, attracting migratory birds, butterflies, and a host of water-loving fauna. Between them the canyon bed looks dry, but in actuality water seeps slowly along through moist gravel a foot or two beneath the surface, readily available with a shovel and a little effort.

The botany and zoology of Fresno Canyon each contain elements of the unexpected. Six varieties of rare plants have been discovered, four of them along Fresno Creek itself. Zone-tailed hawks, golden eagles, and the endangered Mexican duck have been observed. The area is rich in bats whose normal range lies much farther south in Mexico; western mastiff bats and big freetail bats both frequent the vicinity, indicating that colonies may be established nearby. Other species are believed to occur—the spotted bat, which, if bats can be considered beautiful, is considered the most beautiful of bats; and the Mexican long-tongued bat, which feeds upon the nectar of blooming century plants. Because Fresno Creek drains into the Rio Grande, it has provided a historic passageway for bears and mountain lions wandering north from Mexico.

To primitive man, the watered canyon must have seemed a far more attractive home than the arid Solitario. That is not, however, saying much: the nearly three dozen archaeological sites now known suggest a long period of bare subsistence, characterized by foraging and small-game hunting under conditions that made the search for food an almost full-time occupation. There is no evidence that the prehistoric inhabitants of Fresno practiced any sort of agriculture or raised domestic animals. However, they left behind a small collection of simple pictographs. One site, its smoke-blackened roof consisting of a remarkable grooved slab of limestone thrust down as the Solitario was uplifted fifty million years ago, has been decorated with colored handprints. Another depicting men on horseback indicates that Fresno Canyon was inhabited at least until Europeans arrived in the region.

European influence was long confined to the Rio Grande; the white man came late to Fresno Canyon itself. La Junta, now Presidio, was well established when Antonio de Espejo passed through in 1582; and a place called Tapalolmes, near modern-day Redford, was visited by Rábago y Terán in 1747. But Fresno remained untouched. North-south travel, such as there was, flowed for centuries along Alamito Creek, thirty miles northwest of Fresno and nearer to La Junta. This was the route chosen by Espejo on his journey from Santa Fe to the Rio Grande; later it flourished as the Chihuahua Trail, a passageway for American goods before the Civil War and for American cattle after.

Fresno basked in silence until the twentieth century, when a rugged road from Marfa to Lajitas was cut through to give access for the Terlingua mining district. Mule pack trains (immortalized in the photographs of W. D. Smithers) dodged potholes, forded streams, and circumvented rock slides to make the journey in three days. In 1916, when Pancho Villa and his men hid out in Alamito Creek, U.S. Cavalry reinforcements used the primitive Fresno Canyon "highway" to station themselves at Lajitas. Along the route they saw the things we see today: to their right, mountains concealing springs, cool water, and grassy shade; to their left, the Solitario's awesome toothed rim and its three colossal false apertures known as Los Portales.

Beside that road, rancher J. F. Crawford built a home in 1918. The spot he chose was sheltered from north winds by the serrated ridge of Rincon Mountain; it was near a spring, of course. Behind a neat stone wall breached by a wooden gate, he laid down hardwood floors and placed a mantel on his fireplace; outside the living room he built a terraced formal garden with an ornamental pool, and in the back, a citrus orchard. In time the house was bought by Harry Smith, who, like Crawford, raised Angora goats. Smith stayed until the forties, defying climate, predators, and isolation, then sold his land and left.

The Marfa-Lajitas road, now given back to private hands, lies abandoned and impassable through much of Fresno Canyon. The Smith House, as it now is called, is a scene of chilling melancholy. The white man came late to this unconquerable country, and he did not—could not—stay; even the water could not make it his. Nothing is left but the whitewashed

shell; the hardwood floors are gone, the fireplace stripped, the windows carried away, the roof in ruins. Thornbushes clog the decorative pool, while in the orchard one last gnarled orange tree inexplicably survives. Over the door a horseshoe rusts.

132

12

the solitario

Needle Peak

the solitario

Austere, aloof, the vast circular geological uplift called the Solitario lies in splendid isolation twelve miles due north of Lajitas. From the air a casual observer might mistake it for the crater of a meteorite or the collapsed cone of an ancient volcano, so startling is its symmetry. From the ground its jagged limestone rim roils up like a wave of stony whitecaps above the turbulent surface of the Big Bend country.

There is—has always been, since the days of the Spaniards and before—a sense of separateness about the Solitario. One ascends to the brink of this elevated, sloping bowl, eight miles across and sealed inside almost impenetrable walls, expecting that some kind of paradise must surely lie within: if not a lost kingdom, then at least some well-watered, fertile respite from the surrounding countryside. But the allure of Xanadu is an illusion. Unlike the Big Bend's other hidden place, the green and hospitable Chisos Basin, the interior of the Solitario is arid and forbidding. It is a respite from nothing; instead, it recapitulates all the harsh, wild beauty of the uncompromising Chihuahuan Desert.

This portion of Robert Anderson's 320,000-acre Big Bend Ranch is above all else a remarkable geologic library. Few places in Texas relate such a complex terrestrial narrative. Still fewer yield up their secrets so readily. To the practiced eye the story is plain: the torturously folded ancient Paleozoic rocks lying exposed in the Solitario's center; the limestone sifted down by Cretaceous seas and then thrust into a great protective escarpment by the still-unknown forces that uplifted the Solitario dome some fifty million years ago; the lava flows and ash falls of Tertiary time; and the effects of erosion that began, millennia past, when the ancestral Rio Grande began to carve a steady downward course, draining runoff out of the Solitario through four narrow and ever-deepening canyons.

These canyons, locally known as Shutups, provide the only natural passages into the Solitario. (In the north, a primitive road now vaults the rim.) The way is difficult: gradients sometimes reach 400 feet per mile, and the canyon floors are hemmed by walls of limestone and red conglomerate towering as much as 750 feet. In the Lower (or southern) Shutup—the largest, most isolated, and most breathtakingly beautiful of the four—smooth-sided *tinajas* cup deep pools of jade-green water, obstructions or diversions depending upon one's mood. Except in the driest seasons, a shallow flowing stream two or three feet wide meanders over gravel bars between these pools, disappearing and re-emerging as if by whim. But the calm, steep-shadowed serenity of the Shutups is deceiving: floods accompanying late-summer thunderstorms transform them into places of mortal peril, roaring gorges where giant boulders are tumbled about by the current's overwhelming force.

So rugged is the interior of the Solitario that a good day's expedition seldom covers more than fifteen miles, and then only with the aid of a sturdy four-wheel-drive vehicle. To the north, shale lowlands and low sandstone ridges predominate; to the south, volcanic tuff. Characteristic desert grasses, much thinned by grazing, survive in scattered clumps. The black and green chert of the Maravillas formation and the distinctive white rocks of the Caballos Novaculite cap the high ridges rising from the basin floor, constrasting sharply with dark igneous mountains like Needle Peak. Man-made landmarks are few: some scattered tanks, the pump house at Tres Papalotes, and the remote, forgotten Burnt Camp. Permanent surface water is altogether lacking. This is the rawest country known to Texas; to enter the Solitario is to take leave of everything but elemental nature.

Its plant life is, with a few notable exceptions, typical of the Big Bend. Geologic diversity, however, allows species that ordinarily grow in widely separated sites to flourish in proximity to one another. The rim hosts ocotillo, agave, sotol, and desert shrubs like silver-leaf; the interior basin, creosote, mesquite, catclaw acacia; while in the relatively more hospitable Shutups, ash, soapberry, walnut, and buckeye struggle for water in the dry months and cling for life against the periodic torrents. These canyon plants and others like the Havard plum are relics of an earlier age when the climate of the Solitario was cooler and wetter than it is today; they endure in their isolated canyons only because the high cliffs provide shade and shield them from the Solitario's brutal evaporation rate (at ninety inches a year, the highest in the state).

The preeminent botanical treasure of the Solitario is the colony of some forty-five Hinckley oaks clustered together on a low limestone ridge. Except for another small colony near the abandoned mining town of Shafter, these tiny, two-foot-high shrubs are the only known examples of their kind.

Three other plants rare to Texas exist in the Solitario. The Fendler lipfern has been found in a shady side canyon near the Left-hand Shutup. Along the rim, both the night-blooming cereus and the milkwort *Polygala minutifolia* display their distinctive, though quite different, white flowers. *Echinocereus stramineus*, the strawberry pitaya cactus, is by no means either rare or endangered, but its presence in dense profusion along the Solitario's interior slopes is a reassuring sight to epicurean admirers of this, the desert's most delicious edible.

The Solitario's zoology, like its botany, is noteworthy less for any inherent uniqueness than for the way it brings together within a single small area a great variety of normally scattered life forms. One finds familiar vertebrates like kangaroo rats, checkered whiptail lizards, jackrabbits, cottontails, and mockingbirds. More than one hundred species of birds have been identified within the Solitario, among them two rare elf owls seen nesting near Tres Papalotes. The Big Bend gecko, a rare lizard, has been found near the Left-hand Shutup, and leaf-chinned bats are known. The predators of this forty-thousand-acre basin are distinctly different from those that prowl the adjacent countryside. In most of West Texas, man's gradual extermination of large carnivores has left the field to smaller animals like raccoons, skunks, and foxes. In the Solitario the situation is reversed. Cougars and coyotes rule, the rest are scarce or absent. Attracted by the seclusion of this strange, wild place, the cougar has kept its rank in the natural order of things—for how much longer, no one can say.

Waking to a coyote's cry under a canopy of stars, one realizes how far from humankind the Solitario is. From all evidence it has always been so. Nineteen archaeological sites have been identified within its boundaries, some dating back perhaps twelve thousand years; but their contents—scattered lithic tools, fire-cracked rocks, manos, metates, and soot-blackened shelter ceilings—suggest that prehistoric man paid only brief visits in search of food and weapons before returning to the more congenial regions of Fresno and the Bofecillos: a temporary sojourner, nothing more. Its Spanish history is nonexistent. Even the American ranchers, who did not arrive in numbers until the twentieth century, set up their own residences far away. The occasional overnight campsite of the cowhand is man's only recurring modern presence. So far as we know, in twelve thousand years not one permanent human habitation has ever been constructed in the Solitario.

No lost kingdoms here; nothing of the kind was ever seen in this negative oasis. But those who know it best insist it is enchanted, will tell you of strange things that happen on moonless nights, will tell you of the three men who sat in the

half-light of a campfire at Tres Papalotes when a fourth came up and stood by them, all silent, before fading into the shadows. In the Solitario, they will tell you, you always know who else is there; and there were just three men there that night, not four. Who then was the fourth?

Such stories are, one understands, a commonplace of cowboy folklore: the silent stranger who emerges from the dark to share the fire and melts away unseen, an apparition. But somehow they seem more believable out here, in this prickly, hollowed-out cup of earth, inside these fierce excluding walls, where one small campfire crackles vainly against the universal dark. Ghosts, if they be, would surely come.

13

lower canyons
of the
rio grande

San Francisco Canyon

lower canyons of the rio grande

Of all the wild places that remain in Texas, none bears more eloquent witness to the supremacy of nature than the Lower Canyons of the Rio Grande. Prehistoric man struck with them a cautious bargain for sanctuary and sustenance of life. The impatient invading Spaniards, seeking passage through the *despoblado*, put misplaced trust in fragmentary maps and struggled in bewilderment against them for two centuries. Normally self-confident American explorers recoiled with awed respect from the daunting mystery of their cliffs and rapids. Not until 1899 were the canyons fully charted by a scientific expedition, and before 1970 they remained an unknown land to botanists, zoologists, and archaeologists. Even today, this 95-mile ribbon oasis downstream from Big Bend National Park has scarcely changed from the days of the Apaches: its green spring-fed water, its Grecian blue sky, its pale orange bluffs,

147

and the silhouette of a hawk soaring above a dry side canyon define with timeless simplicity the state's most exhilarating wilderness experience.

As the Spaniards and the early Americans found to their dismay, the Lower Canyons are impassable both by land and by any vessel of substantial size. A canoe trip, including portages, requires five to eight days. Once a party has embarked, there is no way out for the duration of the journey. Only a few thousand people have ever made the trip.

Before 1973, most knowledge of the Lower Canyons' biology was conjectural, derived from observations at Black Gap Wildlife Management Area adjacent to the park. Black Gap is still the best place to begin an expedition. Where the Rio Grande meets a tributary called Maravillas, a stony outwash forces it into a channel no wider than a creek; a pebble pitched across eight or ten feet of water will land in Mexico—another sovereignty unmarked by border posts or fences. Lines on maps may show the river as a boundary, but nowhere in these canyons will the canoeist feel any sense of passing along the frontiers of two nations. The river binds together; it does not separate.

Maravillas Canyon reflects the many-layered history of the Big Bend country. Here, in 1852, T. W. Chandler and Duff Green finally abandoned their attempt to survey the rugged boundary from Presidio to Fort Duncan and marched their men, bleeding and discouraged, across northern Mexico to Santa Rosa. Here, for weeks in 1893, Mexican bandits filtered across the river to rustle more than a thousand head of cattle from newly arrived ranchers who lived nearby—including, perhaps, some from the forgotten cowman whose burned adobe house stands now on a promontory among the campsites at Black Gap. Tonight at dusk under a graying sky two old Californians sit in folding chairs outside their curtained camper. A radio stands on a stepladder beside them. It plays rock: not their music, but in the Big Bend, where radio stations are scarce, they are not invited to choose. A tiny fire, hardly bigger than the palm of a hand, burns brightly as they sit with their backs to the towering Mexican mountains. They are the last people we, the canoeists, will see for the next four days.

Downstream from Maravillas Canyon broad terraces, carved 10,000 years ago by an earlier, wider Rio Grande, are visible in the distance across the lowlands known as Outlaw Flats. But soon the walls close in; the river rams against a sheer cliff and swirls at right angles to the solid rock. In the course of a single mile it twists north, east, and south before emerging into the steep-sided chasm called Reagan (or Bullis) Canyon. This is the heartland of the Lower Canyons, a twenty-mile stretch of eastward-flowing water sealed off from the outside world by unscalable escarpments that sometimes reach a thousand feet in height.

The untrained eye perceives them as a sequence of visual delights: barrenness juxtaposed against fertility, white water followed by repose, colors constantly altered by the ever-changing light. But the natural scientist sees methodical order beneath these images; the riverbed, the riverbank, the floodplain terrace, the boulder-covered talus slopes, and the sheer canyon walls capped with aeries. Within this unvarying pattern the life of the wilderness has organized itself.

By the vagaries of nature and by man's indifference, the Lower Canyons remain a wilderness preserve. Relicts of the cooler, wetter Pleistocene continue to exist in their clefts, just as they do in the high altitudes of the Chisos, Davis, and Guadalupe mountains. Birds fleeing the impact of human settlement—herons, eagles, and white-wing doves among them—find sanctuary here, and the highly endangered peregrine falcon almost certainly nests among these crags. The canyons are a refuge for mountain lions and zone-tailed hawks. They are the only known location for the delicate, pink-flowered Maravillas milkwort and the tiny heather leafflower. They are among the few places where the pocketed freetail bat is found. And they provide an irreplaceable corridor through the Chihuahuan Desert for migratory birds. The richness of the canyon life stands in healthy contrast to the adjoining uplands, where overgrazing has devastated the once lush grass.

Midway through Reagan Canyon the human presence

reappears in a setting of unparalleled beauty. Rounding a bend, one sees a minuscule building perched atop the loftiest of cliffs. This is the Asa Jones pump house, where man's ingenuity succeeded in tapping the river through a series of pipes waggling crazily down the canyonside. Abandoned now, the pump house once supplied water for a rustic candelilla-wax-rendering "factory," which, as the story goes, made Asa Jones a millionaire and let him quit this parched desert for the comforts of Alpine.

The pump house serves as a reminder of how few people have ever used the river in modern times. Trappers searched for pelts in the latter part of the nineteenth century. River riders patrolled the banks after World War II to keep diseased animals from crossing north. Sport fishermen occasionally visit the lower end of the canyons today. But the ranchers on the uplands have kept their backs turned resolutely to it; there are lifelong residents of the adjoining property who have never once gazed down from the rim at the twisting green river.

On the grassy alluvial terrace below the Asa Jones pump house, however, it is easy to picture the encampments of Indians who once lived in harmony with the Lower Canyons. Their visits were apparently regular: virtually every habitable site in the Lower Canyons shows some signs of occupation, and archaeologists doubt the canyons were ever completely devoid of human presence in the 10,000 years before the coming of European man. The evidence suggests a hunting-gathering subsistence, the campsites being reoccupied on the Indians' seasonal rounds.

The Indians who visited the Lower Canyons survived on freshwater mussels, land snails, and slow-baked sotol and lechuguilla. They ground the pods of honey mesquite to a pulp and used the flour for flatbreads and porridge. Fruits enlivened mealtimes according to the season, and flavorings for meats like rock squirrel and catfish could be obtained from oregano cimarron and Drummond onions. In the fall the juice of sumac berries, mixed with honey, provided a refreshing drink. To the adventurous visitor willing to live off the land these same foods are available today, along with such modern-day delicacies as white-throated wood rats, chicken-fried.

The hundreds of springs and seeps along the margins of the river not only create a flourishing microhabitat of sedges, rushes, and ferns where canoeists can find reliable supplies of pure water; they also ensure that the Lower Canyons will never be menaced with the extinction that could face the upstream canyons if the Rio Conchos water were cut off. The mean discharge along the Rio Grande increases by nearly a third between Big Bend Park (927 cubic feet per second) and Langtry (1310 cubic feet per second), with most of the difference coming from these springs.

Two miles downstream from Asa Jones' pump house, tucked away beside the rapids formed by the outwash of San Rocendo Canyon, is the least forgettable of all the Lower Canyons' springs: the great "bathtub" hot spring, the oasis of all oases for the weary canoeist. Trapper James McMahon, the first white guide to float the Lower Canyons and live to tell the story, led Robert Hill's 1899 expedition here. Hill, renewed, spent the next half-day soaking in the pool and washing his clothes. Surrounded by a hedge of reeds and floored with sand and smooth-sided pebbles, the sheltered pool is large enough to accommodate three or four bathers in a basin of gushing water. The temperature is warm enough that one does not flinch upon getting in, and cool enough that one never becomes overheated. It is perfection: people often linger for hours, paddling against the current or floating motionless like alligators.

Fourteen miles farther on, at the spectacular cliffs of Burro Bluff, the river again turns north and enters the most arduous stretch of the Lower Canyons. Upper and Lower Madison Falls come in quick succession, to be followed by the perilous but runnable Panther Canyon rapids. One begins to realize how uneasy is the alliance that has been building between canoeist and river in the preceding days; no matter how familiar the waters become, nature and the river remain supreme.

In writing of the Lower Canyons, the temptation is always to particularize: to describe one's own trip, one's own experiences. But what is fundamental is not the particulars but the universal, the abiding river itself. That is what matters, and yet the particulars force themselves onto the page. On the last two nights on the river, these were the particulars:

At the campsite where San Francisco Canyon meets the Rio Grande, a sunset rich with orange, pink, and purple banks of clouds; a driftwood campfire shedding a faint light, like a few candles; canoeists talking softly in small groups, almost in whispers, nothing like the roaring campfire and storytelling of imagination; the mournful harmonica; nightfall with stars and no moon; Taurus, the Pleiades, and over the canyon, Orion setting; the utter peace that bonds men as surely as civilization's ways divide them.

The last night at Pancho's Cave, a rock-shelter high above the river, hastily sought out as a towering thundercloud bears menacingly down above Sanderson Canyon; golfball-size hail covering the ground as if it were a snowfall; in the dry shelter, a dinner brewing in the galley; a thunderstorm with every cliff and crevice in the canyons pouring out its separate waterfall; afterward, a thin sickle moon, stars, and lightning and thunder receding for hours in the east: a pastoral coda.

The float trip ends two miles beyond Pancho's Cave at Dryden Cable Crossing—a historic Rio Grande ford used by the Comanches and Apaches for forays into Mexico. Their trail was a mile wide in places and littered with the skeletons of livestock; it was, marveled one Mexican officer, "so well beaten that it appears that suitable engineers had constructed it." Here one picks up the thread of civilized living with hesitant, blinking eyes. The world has moved a week farther along in its concerns, while one's own life on the river has stayed motionless, like the still point of a turning wheel. One leaves a world where everything is measured by sunrises and sunsets, and returns to a world where the day of the week, and the hour of the day, matter. "Has anyone dropped the Bomb?" a companion asks, and we turn on the car radio to find out.

14

falcon thorn woodland

Prickly Pear

falcon thorn woodland

Disgorged from the turbines of Falcon Dam, the Rio Grande begins its final, sluggish journey to the sea. The great impoundment completed in 1953 is the last barrier to the once-wild waters that have churned their way down from the Big Bend canyons' rapids and cliffs. Beyond the breaks of Starr County the brown river eases, tamed and spiritless, toward the estranging coastal sands.

For a short distance below the dam an isolated remnant of subtropical thorn woodland luxuriates along the riverbank. This brief thicket is one of the few surviving pockets of native vegetation in South Texas. The woodland, its adjacent alluvial terraces, and the chaparral uplands harbor South Texas' most distinctive collection of plant and animal life. Species familiar to northern regions and the western deserts co-exist with others native to Mexico and Central America, many of which

161

reach their northernmost distribution here.

The Mexican burrowing toad and the Mexican white-lipped frog appear in the United States only in Starr and neighboring Hidalgo counties. The poisonous giant toad, which secretes venom through its skin, ranges from the South American tropics to this section of southern Texas. The bird population is so extraordinary that birders from all across the United States make periodic pilgrimages to observe the Falcon avifauna. Twenty-one species of tropical birds come to Falcon and go no farther—attracted, in part, by its tall timber, dense undergrowth, and the few miles of clear water below the dam. Among the notable birds are the brown jay (a native of lowland Mexico and Central America that began nesting at Falcon in the mid seventies), the green jay, the chachalaca, the gray hawk, the hook-billed kite, the black-headed oriole, Lichtenstein's oriole, the olive sparrow, the groove-billed ani, the ferruginous pygmy owl, and the ringed kingfisher.

The botanical treasure of the seven-mile stretch between the dam and the sleepy little town of Salineño is a stand of thirteen Montezuma bald cypresses, the largest of which has a circumference of more than fourteen feet. The drooping coniferous branches of this noble tree are a not-uncommon sight southward into Mexico, but this is the only known grove in the United States. Three other rare plants have been identified in the vicinity of Falcon: Gregg wild buckwheat, previously seen only at one site in Hidalgo County; slashleaf heartseed; and the vivid, orange-petaled *Amoreuxia wrightii*. Texas ebony and anacahuite, less rare, also reach their northern limits here; and natural gardens of peyote, the hallucinogenic holy cactus of the Indians, thrive in Starr County's sandy soil as nowhere else north of the Rio Grande.

Deceptively somnolent by day, Falcon Woodland is transformed after dark. Its night sounds throb with life: the jetlike whine of crickets and katydids, the irregular chorusing of frogs, the insistent buzz of circling mosquitoes, and, of course, the weirdly various calls of night birds. In summer the Lesser Nighthawk darts, batlike, scattering hollow feline purrs; and the pauraque adds a multi-syllabic whistle. Carry a powerful artificial light into the woods at night and meet the enveloping tropics' enigmatic stare: the pauraque's eyes, caught in the beam, shine hot pink; and along the ground, ephemeral phosphorescent mushrooms glow.

Probably no other place in Texas combines such hospitality to plants and animals with such extreme inhospitality to man. William McClintock, passing through the region in the nineteenth century, expressed the definitive truth: "There is nothing of the vegetable world on the Rio Grande, but what is armed with weapons of defense and offense." Even allowing for a certain mellowness along the floodplain itself, this is cruel country—as Cabeza de Vaca found, as Santa Anna found, as anyone finds today traversing it on foot. It is not to be trifled with.

Especially not in summer, when the effective temperature (a combination of humidity, heat, and air movement) is the highest in the United States: worse than Death Valley, comparable to the Red Sea. The wife of an Army officer stationed at Ringgold Barracks (at Rio Grande City) in the 1850's spoke for generations when she declared: "There never was a country more unfitted by nature to be the home of civilized man than this region of the lower Rio Grande of Texas. It seems to hate civilization."

The region has always been a hard and uncomfortable place. The aboriginal Coahuiltecans were nomadic wanderers who wore few clothes, fashioned primitive tools from pink and gold rhyolite, and ate anything their systems could digest— including, if the archaeological evidence is to be believed, substantial quantities of snails. Though related to one another, the Coahuiltecans subsisted in small groups of warring bands, their cultures differing from drainage to drainage across South Texas. As if living out a curse as old as Genesis, they spoke mutually incomprehensible dialects.

By 1840 the Coahuiltecans, stricken by disease and assimilated into the Mexican population, had entirely vanished. The first Spanish explorer, Alonso de Leon, crossed the river in 1686 at Salineño ford, which he called El Cantaro. Official Spanish interest focused elsewhere for several decades, but in the half-century after 1739, successful colonial outposts were established along the south side of the river (among them Camargo, Reynosa, and Meir). Companion settlements on the north side failed; but by 1781, every parcel of riverfront land had been claimed.

Development of the Falcon region, like much of the rest of the Nueces Strip, was delayed by violence and disorder. Indian raids (the last, by Comanches, Kiowas, and Apaches in 1837) were followed by a lawless period of banditry. Mexican invasions of the Republic of Texas were countered by freebooters like Colonel W. S. Fisher, whose Texian force, captured under a flag of truce in 1842 at Meir, was decimated and imprisoned. The establishment of Ringgold Barracks in 1848 was a signal that order would prevail. With occasional lapses, it eventually did. Soon the Roma-Matamoros river run was an important commercial passageway for hides, lead, and wool. In the following century, agriculture and ranching established themselves—less securely in Starr County than elsewhere in the Valley, but sufficiently well to alter the perimeter of Falcon Woodland.

Grasslands have given way to chaparral: nothing remains of the sight that greeted visitors in the 1850's, when grass extended from the river at Rio Grande City to a point sixteen miles inland. With it has gone the water table that sustained the intermittent streams used by the Coahuiltecans. Consequent erosion in the flood-prone arroyos has carried away most, though not yet all, of their pitiful remains.

In recent years the chaparral has in turn given way to quarrying, grazing, and cultivation. Deprived of protective vegetation and assaulted by pesticides, the animal life of the region has undergone profound change. Since mid-century the number and variety of mammals have fallen sharply; the jaguar has disappeared altogether, with the ocelot and the jaguarundi hard on its heels. Such diverse birds as the oliveaceous cormorant, the black hawk, the red-billed pigeon, the tropical parula, the hooded oriole, and the elf owl have been adversely affected by the clearing of the land and by the increased human presence near Falcon Dam.

Man is closing in on the Falcon Woodland. But in the heavy humid heat of a summer afternoon, as blue spiny lizards scramble over the grainy rocks and the pale green branches of Montezuma cypress arc lazily in a gust of wind, he seems as distant as the polar ice.

15

harrison bayou

Hardwood Bottomlands

harrison bayou

Harrison Bayou, a watercourse so slight as scarcely to deserve a name, flows uneventfully for a half-dozen miles through East Texas bottomland forest before spending itself in the shallows of Caddo Lake.

Consider that forest. Once it stretched almost unbroken to the Atlantic. Consider its aboriginal inhabitants the Kadohadacho, kin by culture to the tribes of the eastward-facing woodlands, alien to those of the plains and the open sky. And consider the settlers who in turn supplanted them, conferring names on the humblest streams and ordering the land with methodical precision: from beneath that same canopy they came.

At the beginnings of Texas, this *was* Texas. Eastward lay all manner of familiar things; the rest was an uncertain place. Once Texas belonged to the South, sealed there by terrain of mind as well as land. By its strangeness the forest now confirms how utterly the idea of Texas has changed since Texians themselves first came to be.

Caddo Lake is the largest natural body of fresh water in the state. Legends rooted in the Indian past attribute its formation to some abrupt upheaval of the gods, flooding the sunken earth with a gesture angry or beneficent according to the telling. The truth is more prosaic: over time, the collapse of tree-lined stream banks formed a jam of logs so impenetrable that the waters gradually collected behind the accretion of debris.

The result is less a lake in the conventional sense than a problematic maze where the line dividing land from water is often indistinct. From an irregular expanse of open lake, channels and passageways sluice across the enveloping marsh. "A sequence of concealments and digressions," it has been called, bewildering to the chartless eye. Vegetation and water seem to merge: baldcypress, hyacinth, algae—the vegetation half liquid, the water stirring with hidden greenness below the surface. Clear and fluent, Harrison Bayou is a capillary on this aqueous heart.

Well into the 1830's, the lake and its environs were the domain of Caddo Indians, a loose confederacy of tribes whose bizarre physical appearance seemed preposterously at odds with their intricate hierarchic society. Short of stature and massively tattooed, they purposely deformed their skulls from childhood in furtherance of a now-inscrutable aesthetic. Yet theirs was once a civilization higher than any other in Texas: settled, agricultural, provident; capable of storing its harvests for two years, erecting spacious homes by communal effort, maintaining temples where a symbolic flame was kept perpetually alight. In the end they peaceably yielded their ancestral lands by treaty and embarked on a restless hegira whose misery lasted for most of a century.

That treaty, displayed at the old courthouse in Marshall, foretells their fate in its Latinate cadences. "Goods and horses" to be paid now, it says, then "ten thousand dollars *per annum* for the four years next" if the Caddo will remove themselves from the United States "and never more return to live, settle, or establish themselves as a nation, tribe, or community of people within the same." Like a document negotiated in some baroque drawing room by the plenipotentiaries of European nation-states, it duly bears the witness of its signatories: Jehiel Brooks, for the United States, and the X-marks of 25 illiterate Indian chiefs.

Thus ignobly secured, the Caddo lands became a gateway for migrants from the southern states to Texas. Stern-wheelers and side-wheelers plied the lake itself, following a channel carved by the Big Cypress River which led upstream to the bustling antebellum port of Jefferson. Cargoes waterborne from New Orleans were tagged with playing cards to indicate their destinations, one clue the unlettered stevedores could always fathom: Jefferson the King of Spades, Marshall the King of Diamonds, and on through the deck to lesser towns along the thriving inland waterway. *Floruit* Dixie, for a time; and when the War came, the path of commerce became a lifeline to the beleaguered Confederacy, bearing foodstuffs, cotton, and munitions.

Then as now, Harrison Bayou has remained untouched, curling with quiet inconspicuousness through the forest understory. At fifty feet, it is invisible. Winter sunlight turns the surrounding carpet of damp leaves orange; acorns crunch underfoot. Brush dams built by enterprising beavers stall the swift-flowing water into miniature lakes, imitating Caddo.

Around the Bayou lie three hundred acres of virgin bottomland hardwoods, the finest stand in Texas. Their isolation saved them from the logger's axe; their nearness to Caddo saved them from inundation by any man-made reservoir. Now they are fenced within the Longhorn Army Ammunition Plant, immune to harvest. In this protected circle are the state's largest water hickory and flowering dogwood, along with huge persimmon, overcup oak, water locust, water elm, and hawthorn. Flanged baldcypresses tower above the Bayou—the sort of trees that foresters gaze upon and lovingly compute board-feet. Around the lesser hardwoods wind sinewy vines, adhesive, serpentine.

On the sandy ridges, the transition to pine forest is immediate: as moisture and soil conditions change by inches, so too does vegetation. Gray squirrels romp through the treetops as if in festival; bobcat, mink, and feral pig abound beneath the hardwoods. Twenty-nine species of snakes have been recorded nearby, including one, the mud snake, which eats nothing except an eel-like amphibian called siren.

Harrison Bayou is a haven for bottomland birds. The elusive ivory-billed woodpecker may conceivably be here, though no clear proof of its existence has been found. But even in January its woodpecker kin are present, drumming across the leafless distances, interrupted by the more insistent resonance of locomotives on the nearby main line of the Kansas City Southern. Those whistles cut through a woodland idyll like a knife, reminders of old Jefferson, a town brought low by the railroad.

When the ancient log jam that sustained the lake was cleared away by Army Engineers in 1873, no community associated with the Caddo region saw its fortunes plummet more quickly than Jefferson. A replacement dam built to restore the level of the lake failed to regenerate its commerce; and Jefferson, stiff-necked and proud, spurned the vulgar railroads whose smoky, raucous presence might have saved the town. "This is the end of Jefferson," warned the president of the Texas & Pacific, and the railroads proliferated in more compliant places, co-opting Jefferson's fruitful hinterlands.

From a population of 30,000 in its prime, the town within a decade went to decay. In the numbed judgment of its local newspaper, the *Jimplecute*, "our people continued to lie still and watch, having been made too confident by a long prosperity." By 1888 the railroad's fierce example has been made, *in terrorem*: Jefferson was a skeleton of itself, a town hanged in irons on a gibbet.

Today, despite much fashionable restoration, the remnant of the city seems—not *brooding* exactly, but *meditating* on those days of its vanished glories. The platted streets betray the framework of a far larger town, stranding homes among too many telltale vacant lots. Contemporary Jefferson has the

slightly abashed air of one who bravely stood up for a principle only to discover that it was the wrong principle.

In this it is like the South itself, whose legacy is kept with the rest of Jefferson's past in the town museum.

There the curators preside over collections of Confederate memorabilia. Relics which not so many years ago shimmered with the respect owed to noble causes now seem invested with unadmitted shame: preserved long after the popular faith that such things matter has dissolved, their light dusting of embarrassment deepens with each passing year.

Like the Texas that once was steeped in Southern ways, the museum in Jefferson seems less a memorial to the Confederacy than its mausoleum, a kind of graveyard where dis-

175

quieting memories lie visibly interred: too recent to remove, too burdened with ambiguities of conscience to revere. Those Texians are strangers to us now.

> *Row after row with strict impunity*
> *The headstones yield their names to the element*
> *The wind whirrs without recollection. . . .*

Eastward the meandering Big Cypress rolls untenanted to Caddo Lake. Where once low fields of cotton prospered on land laboriously cleared, now spindly pine plantations rise in geometric lines; at man's behest the shadowed forest reclaims its own.

> *Turn your eyes to the immoderate past,*
> *Turn to the inscrutable infantry rising*
> *Demons out of the earth—they will not last.*
>
> *Now that the salt of their blood*
> *Stiffens the saltier oblivion of the sea . . .*
> *What shall we say of the bones, unclean,*
> *Whose verdurous anonymity will grow?*
> *The ragged arms, the ragged heads and eyes*
> *Lost in these acres of the insane green?*[1]

---

[1]Excerpt from "Ode to the Confederate Dead" from COLLECTED POEMS 1919–1976 by Allen Tate. Copyright 1937 by Charles Scribner's Sons. Copyright 1977 by Allen Tate. Reprinted by permission of Farrar, Straus and Giroux, Inc.

16

salt flats

The Flats

salt flats

The descent from the gusty elevations of Guadalupe Pass westward onto the level desert floor is one of the sharpest transitions in Texas. One hundred and twenty-five years ago, weary travelers who had successfully negotiated the treacherous rocky shelves and steep gorges of the pass—a journey that could take six heart-stopping hours—peered ahead into the afternoon sun to admire what seemed to be a huge and welcoming lake. But the waters were a mirage. And the journey ahead often proved more perilous than the one their tottering wagons had completed.

Along the western edge of the Guadalupe escarpment lie the Salt Flats: playas and dunes formed by peculiar currents of the prevailing winds. Except for brief periods after heavy rains, the lake beds are dry; their deposits of salt glisten white and deceiving under the beating sun. Today's travelers speed by with scarcely an indifferent glance, but the place they skirt so casually has shaped the life of this corner of Texas for hundreds of years.

The dry lakes themselves, the playas, are nearly sterile. Only simple crustaceans like brine shrimp can survive their dense concentrations of desiccating salt, lying dormant through long dry spells and bursting forth into frenzied activity after a rain. Fringing the playas are sloping basins of pickleweed and grasses. Beyond them soar range upon range of dunes, upswept patterns of powdery white gypsum and fine red quartzite sand. This is the quintessence of desert.

The sand grows coarser as the land closes upon the Guadalupe range, grading into typical southwestern bajada country riven with arroyos that are choked with shrubs. The great bluffs and mountain peaks rising steeply in the background separate this stark landscape from the cool, well-watered highlands of McKittrick Canyon, with its maples and madrones, its alligator juniper and rainbow trout, just fourteen miles away.

The quest for salt as a condiment and a preservative has been a persistent thread of human history. At least one thousand years ago, primitive hunters and gatherers frequented the Salt Flats. Their campsites have been found in more than four dozen places along the shores. Mescalero Apaches, who may have considered the salt deposits sacred, used them regularly. When the focus of Spanish empire shifted southward to El Paso del Norte after the Pueblo Revolt of 1680, two governors dispatched expeditions to find the fabled beds of salt. That both should have failed is a measure of the remoteness of the country, the austerity of the desolate land, and the unyielding menace of the Apaches. Though the Salt Flats' existence was well known by word of mouth, not until the 1740's did their location appear on maps. And despite their lavishness—in places the deposits lay six inches thick along the surface, pure salt—the gain to be had by reaching them impressed many adventurers as scarcely worth the risk.

Those who came had no incentive to linger. They shoveled up as much as their wagons could bear and creaked warily back to the safety of El Paso. Few, it seems fair to assume, paused to explore the mysterious solitude of the adjacent dunes. Like a changing, changeless river, these dunes are now as they were then: building, unbuilding, and rebuilding themselves invisibly to the eye. Their sweeping Moorish curves, their ridges sharp as scimitars, the ribbed patterns on the surface of the sand, seem almost sanctified, the placement of each single grain dictated to perfection by the wind. Their abstract beauty testifies to the driving geometry of nature.

The *despoblado* of western Texas was for generations the most stubborn obstacle to travel between San Antonio and El Paso. Searching for a safe route, Major Robert Neighbors led a party eastward in 1849 from El Paso through Hueco Tanks, the Salt Flats, and Guadalupe Pass. Gold-seekers bound for California soon adopted the route. The Salt Flats entered upon their one fleeting moment of glory as a pathway to the Pacific. By 1853 regular traffic flowed along the Neighbors trail even though whole parties sometimes became stranded in the waterless reaches near the Flats. By 1858 the Butterfield Overland Mail Company had instituted stagecoach service on this, the "Ox-Bow Route." But within a year Butterfield, frustrated by Indian attacks and the risks of travel through the arid country, moved its line south. The glory had lasted less than ten years.

Never again would the passage through the Salt Flats and Guadalupe Pass hold such significance. Mostly it was a way strewn with hardships, the kind of place where travelers stopped to add stones and a prayer to the simple trailside graves of others who had gone before. But it had the exhilarating freshness and purity of newly opened land. No doubt many felt the same emotions as John Russell Bartlett, the first boundary commissioner, who watched a sunrise on Guadalupe Peak in 1850 and wrote in awe, "No painter's art could reproduce, or colors imitate, these gorgeous prismatic tints."

The Salt Flats figured one last time in the affairs of West Texas. Under Spanish law, their deposits had been deemed held in common for the use of all; when in due course under

Texas law the land was acquired by private owners who proposed to charge a fee, conflict broke out over the disposition of the salt. Eventually it exploded beyond the issues of immemorial custom versus private rights and engaged El Paso politics, racial animosities, and federal troops. The Salt War of 1877 was the climactic moment in the history of the Salt Flats. Within six years afterward, the Indians had been driven into submission, the railroad had gone through, and commerce flowed safely across the *despoblado*. The unique value of the Salt Flats was at an end. Having supplied a vital resource for as long as men had known of them, they became abruptly inessential. Ours is the first century in which men can pass them by, indifferent.

Today the Salt Flats show the scars of human contact. Heavy grazing in the bajada has altered the balance of the soil, allowing creosote bush to infest the area. Sport riders on motorcycles churn up the dunes for weekend amusement. But the basic elements are unchanged: fierce extremes of temperature (ranging from 105 degrees to minus 2 degrees) and of precipitation, which comes in torrents when it comes. Among the white gypsum dunes some plants of limited distribution survive, including the gyp daisy, the pitchfork, and Warnock's groundsel; and unusual white lizards like *Holbrookia maculata* can be found.

Overshadowed by the sheltering mountains, the Flats no longer exert the magnetic attraction that drew numberless generations to them. The surrounding land can no longer be regarded as pristine. But the haunting dunes remain, images outside of time.

17

quitman mountains

Spanish Dagger

Quitman Mountains

Angling broadly southeastward from the Hudspeth County seat of Sierra Blanca, Red Light Draw divides the Eagle Mountains from the Quitman Mountains like a dry sea bed between two continents.

Tradition says the draw was named for the signals affixed to its windmills many years ago as an aid to aircraft navigation. Earlier travelers doubtless would have welcomed an airplane as the only sensible means of crossing this uncharitable Chihuahuan Desert. Stagecoach companies like Butterfield and the Jackass Mail endured the Indian attacks and the lack of water, but they left the draw and sought the relative safety of the river at the first usable pass—a place now known as Quitman Gap but called then, with both more poetry and more exactitude, Puerto de los Lamentos.

The "pass of lamentations" has not changed. It is the sort

of place one would take a European visitor who asked to see the real West, not the West of Hollywood imagination. Its scale is modest. The high peaks are set far back, and the winding trail hugs the contours of the earth, rising and falling deceptively among low, knobby hills. Yucca and cactus loom on the rocky slopes like standing Indians. Afternoon shadows gather early. The air breathes ambush.

By 1859 Quitman Gap had succeeded the Salt Flats as the riskiest section of the San Antonio–El Paso road. A small post near the river, Fort Quitman, was garrisoned intermittently and largely ineffectively until 1876, when it was reduced to a stage stop. Apache skirmishes persisted in the Quitmans after such hazards had become but a memory elsewhere. In the summer of 1880 a stagecoach carrying a retired general, J. J. Byrne, was pursued for five miles through the pass. The carriage was left with twenty bullet holes and the general with an unenviable niche in the history books as the last passenger killed by Indians in Texas.

Downstream from the meager remains of the shabby fort, the 6700-foot Quitman range verges diagonally ever closer to the Rio Grande, tapering to a cul-de-sac at Indian Hot Springs. The range intrigues geologists for its contrasts. The northern end is a granitic moonscape of Tertiary igneous rocks; the southern is jagged and deep Cretaceous limestone.

The river below the springs is a surprisingly languid place. Sunlight dapples the water beneath thickets of salt cedar. Surrounded by the buzz of insects, hearing the occasional splash of a fish, watching the myriad ants busy themselves alongside fallen logs, one can imagine this to be the tropics instead of the nearly rainless desert that lies beyond the trees.

Further on, the river swirls into the shallow, bubbling rapids of Mayfield Canyon. The reach of the Rio Grande from Fort Quitman to Presidio has always been reckoned its least consequential part. When the first Spanish explorers, Chamuscado and Rodriguez, struggled through the difficult terrain in 1581, they encountered a few Indians using the riverbank seasonally, but no farm villages. The river was too untrustworthy for that. Until its flow was tamed by dams in 1915, prolonged dry spells were broken by all-consuming floods. Mexican pioneer settlements founded in the 1820's dwindled steadily until, by 1880, the valley near the Quitmans was again unpopulated. Farms introduced after the construction of the twentieth-century dams have followed the same bleak cycle of decline: because of upstream irrigation and El Paso's municipal demands, the river reaches Presidio (if at all) carrying one-tenth of its pre-1915 flow. In 1902 it averaged thirteen feet deep above Presidio; by the 1980's, a mere three feet.

Even this shrunken river may soon disappear into a man-made trough. The International Boundary and Water Commission, discomfited by the Rio Grande's tendency to meander without regard to lawful borders, has begun to dredge 170 miles of river between Presidio and Fort Quitman. And the wild solitude may be broken for good if petroleum is discovered in the Texas Overthrust, a geologic formation encompassing the territory from Candelaria to Sierra Blanca, now being mapped and poked by optimistic speculators.

At least until the Overthrust erupts with oil, the most noteworthy site in the Quitman Mountains is the set of six thermal pools known collectively as Indian Hot Springs. Their reputation for curative powers made them fleetingly popular as a health resort in the 1930's. Frank X. Tolbert, the dean of modern-day Texas explorers, has been visiting the springs for more than thirty years and records that they have entertained such politically diverse bathers as Pancho Villa and H. L. Hunt. Hunt even bought the property in the 1960's, and although it has again changed hands, evidence of his attentions is apparent in the cottages, the unoccupied thirteen-room hotel, and the covered enclosure for the most important pool.

One visitor, though, paused at the springs for something more than a leisurely medicinal soak. The Apache chief Victorio camped there during the final furious twilight of the Texas Indian wars, following a battle with a detachment of Buffalo Soldiers, the renowned Negro cavalry troops who bore the brunt of responsibility for protecting the borderlands. Some say the soldiers got their name from the buffalo skins they wore; others say their appearance reminded the Indians of buffalo. They often ranged hundreds of miles from their base at Fort Davis. One such group, returning from a week's patrol along the river in 1880, was surprised at dawn by Victorio's followers on a hill above the springs. Their fate is one of the enduring legends of the Quitman Mountains.

The soldiers hurriedly piled together a desperate redoubt. It can still be seen: a low semicircle of rocks, twenty-seven feet wide, eighteen feet from back to front, open at the rear where a steep hill afforded natural protection.

At this spot the Buffalo Soldiers made their stand. It is said the Apaches approached them patiently, rolling boulders ahead as shields. Here and there in the gravel a spent cartridge lies, touched by no other hands since a doomed soldier placed it in his rifle. Five of the six were killed; one escaped. As if to hold back the force the soldiers represented, the Apaches drove tent pegs through the bodies of the dead.

Who were these six, and what must they have thought under that broad sky, in this barren place, cornered? It is fair to suppose that some had been born to slavery and could remember other ways in the black-earth delta or the cool Shenandoah. Some perhaps had heard tales of lives stranger still in the green West African savannah. The unfolding of generations had brought them far from familiar things to die alone in this inexplicable desolation.

The ground on the hill being much too hard for graves, the Buffalo Soldiers were buried in a low alluvial wash beside an Indian spring. Their grim cairns, unmarked and angular as coffins, were layered with smooth mortar to secure the rocks against the elements; but the wind and sun have had their way, and the mortar does not hold.

For the Apaches the victory was transient. Within a few months they were defeated forever in the battle of Victorio Canyon, and the railroad clanged down on the pacified land at Sierra Blanca. Exactly three hundred years after the first curious Europeans had appeared, the contest for the land was over.

Another hundred years, and portions of the river and the mountains are much transformed by man. The fine thick grama grass that once covered the hillsides is gone from the lower slopes; in its stead are the motley shrubs that follow overgrazing. Prolific salt cedars, purposely introduced from abroad for erosion control during the first third of the twentieth century, have attracted white-winged doves to a region foreign to them just forty years ago. Even the bullfrogs and carp are newcomers that would have been unfamiliar to a cavalry patrol.

In three centuries the Quitmans passed from savagery to conquest. In the fourth they were secured by the civilization of which they had become a part. These years were witness to the ebb and flow, ceaseless and continuing, of peoples across the face of the earth. For a thousand years before 1581, the customs and techniques and forms of thought of those who lived here could have been recognized by their ancestors or their descendants ten generations removed. But no longer: today the Quitmans are a minor annex of an altogether different culture; and those who live here possess more kinship with the mind of distant Europe than with the lost mysteries of Jumano, Patarabueye, Apache, or Comanche. The history of the Quitmans seems unremarkable only because its central fact is the same as America's central fact.

How did Europe come to Red Light Draw? What keeps it there? Riding homeward along the dusty road, one is prompted to consider how civilizations seed themselves in distant places, taking root in some and withering in others. Four hundred years have severed Red Light Draw from the world it had known immemorially, sealing it to another whose roots twine through Latin odes and English meadows. Can it thrive there, in land so harsh that mortar does not hold?

INDEX

207